GROUNDED DESIGNS FOR

ONLINE AND HYBRID LEARNING

ONLINE AND HYBRID LEARNING TRENDS AND TECHNOLOGIES

EDITED BY ATSUSI "2C" HIRUMI

International Society for Technology in Education
EUGENE, OREGON • WASHINGTON, DC

Grounded Designs for Online and Hybrid Learning Series
Online and Hybrid Learning Trends and Technologies
Edited by Atsusi "2C" Hirumi

Production Editor: *Lynda Gansel*
Production Coordinator: *Emily Reed*
Copy Editor: *Kathy Hamman*
Proofreader: *Ann Skaugset*
Indexer: *Wendy Allex*
Cover Design: *Tamra Holmes*
Book Design and Production: *Kim McGovern*

Library of Congress Cataloging-in-Publication Data

Online and hybrid learning trends and technologies / edited by Atsusi "2C" Hirumi.
    pages cm. — (Grounded designs for online and hybrid learning series)
  Includes bibliographical references and index.
  ISBN 978-1-56484-337-1 (pbk. : alk. paper)
  1. Blended learning. 2. Computer-assisted instruction. 3. Distance education.
   4. Education, Secondary—Computer-assisted instruction. 5. Educational technology.
   I. Hirumi, Atsusi editor of compilation.
  LB1028.3.O5516 2014
  371.3—dc23

                                                              2013043586

First Edition
ISBN: 978-1-56484-337-1 (paperback)
ISBN: 978-1-56484-487-3 (e-book)

Printed in the United States of America

Cover Art: © Fotolia.com/radoma

ISTE® is a registered trademark of the International Society for Technology in Education.

FSC
www.fsc.org
MIX
Paper from
responsible sources
FSC® C014174

About ISTE

The International Society for Technology in Education is the premier membership association for educators and education leaders committed to empowering connected learners in a connected world. Home to the ISTE Conference and Expo and the widely adopted ISTE Standards for learning, teaching, and leading in the digital age, the association represents more than 100,000 professionals worldwide.

We support our members with professional development, networking opportunities, advocacy, and ed tech resources to help advance the transformation of education. To find out more about these and other ISTE initiatives, visit iste.org.

As part of our mission, ISTE works with experienced educators to develop and publish practical resources for classroom teachers, teacher educators and technology leaders. Every manuscript we select for publication is carefully peer reviewed and professionally edited.

About the Editor and Authors

 Editor and contributor **Atsusi "2c" Hirumi** is an associate professor in the Instructional Design and Technology program at the University of Central Florida (UCF). Born in New York, Hirumi spent most of his formative years growing up in Nairobi, Kenya, where he went to middle school and high school at the International School of Kenya. He earned a bachelor's degree in science education at Purdue University, a master's degree in educational technology at San Diego State University, and a doctorate in instructional systems at Florida State University. He earned tenure and promotion to associate professor at the University of Houston-Clear Lake before moving to the University of Central Florida in 2003.

Since 1995, Hirumi has centered his teaching, research, and service on the design of online and hybrid learning environments. At UHCL and UCF, Hirumi led efforts to transform entire certificate and master's degree programs in Instructional Design & Technology for totally online and hybrid course delivery. He has also worked with universities, community colleges, K–12 school districts, medical centers, and the military across North America, South America, and the Middle East to establish online and hybrid training programs, courses, and degree programs. For the past five years, Hirumi has focused his research and development on using story, play, and games to evoke emotions and spark the imagination to enhance experiential learning. He is currently working with colleagues to examine the neurobiological foundations for experiential learning and to develop, test, and refine the InterPLAY instructional theory to guide the design of experiential learning landscapes.

Based on his work, Hirumi has published 28 refereed journal articles, 16 book chapters, and has made more than 100 presentations at international, national, and state conferences on related topics. He also recently edited the book *Playing Games in Schools: Video Games and Simulations for Primary and Secondary Education* published by ISTE. Awards include the Army Training DL Maverick Award for leadership in distance learning, the Texas Distance Learning Association award for Commitment to Excellence and Innovation, the WebCT Exemplary Online Course Award, the University of Houston-Clear Lake Star Faculty Award, the Phi Delta Kappa Outstanding Practitioner Award, the ENRON Award for Innovation, and a second place Award for Excellence for an electronic performance support system designed to help faculty develop and deliver interactive television courses.

Dedication

This book and the entire series is dedicated to all of my students and colleagues who pushed me to put the information and insights I had on e-learning into a book. Thank you for your encouragement and ongoing support. I hope I can continue to inspire, and to offer new and useful perspectives on teaching, learning, and instructional design.

Chapter Authors

Michael Barbour has been active in the K–12 online learning movement for almost a decade. In 1999 he was tasked with the creation of a multi-district virtual schooling initiative that focused upon Advanced Placement (AP) social studies courses. Since this time he has developed and taught courses for virtual schools and private course vendors in Newfoundland and Labrador, Illinois, and Michigan. He has held administrative positions in both province-wide and private virtual schools. At present, Michael continues to co-teach the AP European History course for the Illinois Virtual High School. In addition to his practical experience, Michael has been an avid scholar in this growing field. He has been responsible for leading more than a dozen research projects in Canada and the United States into a variety of issues pertaining to K–12 online learning. From this research Michael has published more than twenty articles and given over forty presentations on this topic.

Zane L. Berge, PhD, is a professor and former director of the Training Systems graduate programs at the UMBC campus, University of Maryland System. He teaches graduate courses involving training in the workplace and distance education. Prior to UMBC, Berge was founder and director of the Center for Teaching and Technology, Academic Computer Center, Georgetown University, Washington, DC. It was there that he first combined his background in business with educational technology to work in the areas of online journals, moderated online discussion lists, and online education and training. Berge's publications include work as a primary author, editor, or presenter of 12 books and over 300 book chapters, articles, conference presentations, and invited speeches worldwide.

John H. Curry, PhD, is an assistant professor of educational technology at Morehead State University in Morehead, Kentucky. He uses podcasting in every class he teaches, and he has coordinated the podcasting of major technology conferences. His research interests include multimedia design and development, the integration of technology into teaching, and distance education. He earned a PhD in Instructional Technology and an MA in the Theory and Practice of Writing from Utah State University, and a BA in English from Brigham Young University. But his most cherished accomplishment is his family. He has been happily married for more than twenty years to his wife, Lori, and is the father of four children: John, Natalie, Andrew, and Emma.

Richard Hartshorne is an associate professor of educational technology at the University of Central Florida (UCF). He earned his PhD in Curriculum and Instruction from the University of Florida, with specializations in Technology and Teacher Education and Educational Technology Production. At UCF, his teaching focuses on the integration of technology into the educational landscape, as well as instructional design and development. Prior to his tenure at UCF, he served as an assistant and associate professor of instructional systems technology at the University of North Carolina at Charlotte, as well as a high school physics teacher. His research interests primarily involve the production and effective integration of instructional technology into the teaching and learning environment. More specifically, his major areas of research interest are rooted in issues influencing effective teaching and learning in online environments, the integration and role of technology in teacher education, and factors that influence the effectiveness and integration of emerging technology into the K–post-secondary curriculum. Hartshorne has presented at more than 50 state, national, and international conferences, and published numerous book chapters and articles in refereed journals, on a variety of educational technology topics, including Web 2.0 tools in teaching, learning, and knowledge management, MMORPGs, and citizenship education, and the remote observation of preservice teachers.

Kathryn Kennedy is an assistant professor of instructional technology at Georgia Southern University. This is her fifth year researching K–12 online learning and eighth year studying distance learning in general. She holds a PhD from the University of Florida in curriculum and instruction, with a concentration in educational technology, a master's from Florida State University in library and information science, specializing in young adult literature, and a Bachelor of Arts from the University of Florida in English, with an emphasis in children's and adolescent literature. Her practical experience includes being a pre-service and in-service teacher, technology specialist, and library/media center specialist. Her research interests include professional development for technology integration and instructional design in traditional, blended, and online learning environments.

John Neely is the director of learning solutions at Oak Grove Technologies. For the past 15 years he has led technology-based learning and development projects, primarily for federal government agencies such as the U.S. Departments of Education, Labor, Health and Human Services, and Housing and Urban Development. Before joining Oak Grove, Neely was the learning and development manager at an IT services company with 7,000 employees, with responsibility for supporting strategic business initiatives in major focus areas of compliance training, leadership and management development, technology training, and soft skills development. He has an MA in Instructional Systems Development from the University of Maryland Baltimore County and a BA in History from the College of Wooster, Ohio.

Contents

Contents

Introduction

Atsusi "2c" Hirumi

Many different trends and issues face educators and instructional designers seeking to facilitate e-learning through the design and delivery of online or hybrid learning environments. In this three-book series, titled Grounded Designs for Online and Hybrid Learning, the first book, *Online and Hybrid Learning Design Fundamentals,* covers basic tasks for systematically designing online and hybrid coursework. The first book illustrates methods for aligning learner assessments to learning objectives, presents a framework for designing and sequencing meaningful e-learning interactions, and provides tactics for searching vast repositories of existing, sharable content objects to reduce costs and facilitate the development of e-learning materials. It also compares Web 2.0 with prior technologies used to facilitate e-learning, offers practical tools for preparing students for successful online learning, interprets laws and provides examples of how online instruction could and should be universally designed for children with special needs and concludes by discussing how e-learning may be designed and delivered to meet ISTE's National Educational Technology Standards (NETS) for teachers and students.

The second book in the series, *Online and Hybrid Learning Designs in Action,* stresses the importance of grounding the design of online and hybrid learning environments. Based on cognitive information processing, inquiry, and experiential and game-based theories of teaching and learning, it provides concrete examples of totally online and hybrid lessons to illustrate the application of eight different instructional strategies: Gagné's Nine Events of Instruction, WebQuests, the 5E Instructional Model, VeeMaps, Authentic Historical Investigations, Guided Experiential Learning, the Inter*PLAY* instructional strategy, and Game-Based Learning Principles.

This third book in the series, *Online and Hybrid Learning Trends and Technologies,* looks further into several key areas that I've found of interest and value for designing online and hybrid learning environments. In Chapter 1, Richard Hartshorne gives examples of five pedagogical approaches and five technological tools for managing large online courses. Then, in Chapter 2, John Curry discusses practices and precautions for podcasting and provides information and links to examples of K–12 podcasts, as well as resources for creating podcasts, hosting podcasts, and integrating free music resources into podcasts. For Chapter 3, John Neely and Zane Berge look at the use of virtual worlds for engaging learners, encouraging collaboration, promoting self-directed exploration, and facilitating student-led, informal learning. Finally, in Chapter 4, Michael Barbour and Kathryn Kennedy show the reach of e-learning and contrast what's happening across the globe by exploring the state of K–12 online learning in the United States, Canada, Mexico, Australia, New Zealand, Singapore, South Korea, and Turkey.

This three-book series is written primarily for K–12 educators, including teachers and administrators, and for instructional designers who may be creating educational materials for K–12 online and hybrid courses. However, if you teach in a college or university setting or design educational and training materials for higher education or business and industry, I think you'll find that the fundamental principles, processes, and examples covered in these books offer insights for and apply to the design of e-learning environments across settings.

All three books are based on three fundamental premises. To increase quality (reduce variance) and design effective, efficient, and engaging online and hybrid courses, educators and course designers should make sure that they: (a) ground the design of their coursework on research and theory; (b) follow a systematic design process to align basic elements of instruction (namely, objectives, assessments, and instructional strategy); and (c) think and, whenever possible, act systemically to ensure all necessary components of the educational system are aligned and work together to facilitate e-learning.

Grounded Design

Grounded design is defined as "the systematic implementation of processes and procedures that are rooted in established theory and research in human learning" (Hannafin, Hannafin, & Land, 1997, p. 102). Grounded design articulates and aligns theory with practice for the purpose of optimizing learning. Regardless of your underlying educational values and beliefs, grounded design provides a procedure that you can use in a variety of settings.

To facilitate the process, Hannifin et al. (1997) posit four criteria for grounded design, including:

- ▶ The application of a defensible theoretical framework clearly distinguishable from other perspectives,

- ▶ The use of methods that are consistent with the outcomes of the research conducted,

- ▶ The ability to generalize beyond one particular instructional setting or problem, and

- ▶ Iterative validation through successive implementations.

Addressing these criteria will give you a solid foundation for designing coursework and for improving your methods and materials over time. However, grounding the design of your lessons and courses does not necessarily guarantee that your students will achieve targeted outcomes in an effective and efficient manner. A number of tasks must be completed before and after you design your course to facilitate e-learning.

Systematic Design

To create an online or hybrid course, you may or may not follow a systematic design process. Those who carry through a systematic process use the results of one task as input for subsequent tasks. For instance, an educator or instructional designer, following a systematic process, may gather and use these data as input to accomplish each task sequentially: at the outset of the course, assess the students' performance levels and analyze the results to identify the essential skills and knowledge they have not mastered; use these skills and knowledge to generate, cluster, and sequence objectives; employ the objectives to define and align learner assessments; apply the objectives and assessments to formulate an instructional strategy; and utilize the strategy to select tools and technologies for facilitating achievement of the objectives.

Vital to long-term learning of skills and knowledge for these reasons, systematic design:

Begins with an analysis of the target learners and desired learning outcomes.
Such analyses are necessary for proper planning and decision making. Without these,
key instructional components may be missing or misaligned.

Provides clear linkages between design tasks. The resulting alignment among
instructional objectives, strategies, and assessments is essential for facilitating
learning in online, hybrid, and conventional classroom learning environments.

Is based on a combination of practical experience, theory, and research. Key design
decisions are informed by what is known about human learning, instruction, and
emerging technologies to avoid haphazard investments in unsubstantiated fads
or opinions.

Is empirical and replicable. To increase returns on investment, instructional materials
are designed to be used more than once with as many learners as possible. The costs
associated with systematic design are worth the investment because the resulting
materials are reusable.

Is generalizable across delivery systems. The resulting materials may be used
to support the delivery of instruction in conventional, hybrid, and totally online
learning environments.

A number of limitations are also associated with systematic design. For instance, systematic
design takes time and expertise—vital human resources that can be spent on other projects.
Educators and instructional designers are rarely given enough time and support to adhere to
a systematic design process. Interim products (e.g., paper-based design documents) are not
flashy and may not capture the attention of key stakeholders who are important for supporting
designers and their efforts.

Many also associate systematic design with ADDIE (analysis, design, development, implementation, and evaluation), a well-known model for producing training and educational programs.
The military and corporations have used the ADDIE model successfully across the United States
and around the world for decades. Variations of ADDIE (see, for examples, Dick, Carey, & Carey,
2009; Smith & Ragan, 1999) continue to be adopted by educators and instructional designers to
produce educational and training materials in a systematic fashion for the reasons mentioned
earlier. Critics of ADDIE, however, argue that it is too linear, too time-consuming, too resource
intensive, and too inflexible, failing to accommodate changes in learners' needs and instructional
materials during development and delivery. Critics also point to poorly designed instructional
materials said to be based on the ADDIE process that are not effective, efficient, or engaging.
Yet, experienced instructional designers realize that more often than not, ineffective, inefficient,
and unappealing instruction result from inappropriate or inadequate applications of ADDIE
(e.g., people cutting corners due to lack of time, training, or resources) rather than inherent
problems with the model itself. ADDIE also does not have to be applied in a linear fashion,
which is a common myth; spiral and other iterative models of ADDIE are widespread.

Experts now advocate what are referred to as agile approaches to design, such as the successive approximation model (SAM) that further accentuates the iterative and collaborative nature of design (Allen, 2012). Figure I.1 depicts what Allen refers to as the extended successive approximation model (SAM2) for projects that require significant content or e-learning development and more advanced programming.

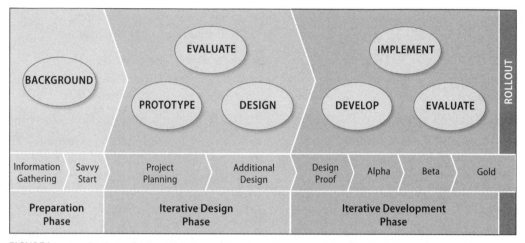

FIGURE I.1 ▶ The three-phase extended successive approximation model or SAM2 *(This figure is reprinted from Allen, 2012, with permission from ASTD Press.)*

Whether you use ADDIE, SAM, or other processes, it is important to remember that a focus on tangible results without sufficient planning or testing may result in a false sense of economy. The impact of poorly designed lessons may not be evident until aspiring learners are asked to perform key tasks for which they are not prepared. Dissatisfied learners may also drop out and warn others to avoid your program. The bottom line is that you should use a process that ensures the alignment of objectives, instructional strategies, and assessment, which leads to the development of instructional materials that consistently result in desired learning outcomes on time and within budget. Systematic design (as discussed in this series' first book and as advocated in the second and third books) helps ensure alignment between and among fundamental instructional elements and reduces variance of quality without inhibiting educators' and instructional designers' creativity if applied in an appropriate manner. Nevertheless, grounded and systematic design may still not be sufficient for ensuring that all students achieve your targeted learning outcomes.

Systemic Thinking and Action

Well-designed instructional materials and coursework are essential but not necessarily sufficient for facilitating e-learning. In an online environment, an instructor may not be readily available to fill in gaps and make up for inadequacies in the instructional materials. Students may not be able to drop what they are doing to meet with advisors to address logistical issues. If some students cannot readily register for and access coursework, acquire materials, submit assignments, obtain feedback, receive advisement, access technical support, and otherwise navigate the training or educational system, it doesn't matter how excellent the instructional materials are because learning may not occur. Students may actually prefer an online program with high-quality student services (user-friendly; convenient; and responsive to learners' requests by advisors, tech support personnel, and instructors) and mediocre course materials to a program with mediocre student services and high-quality online coursework. In these ways, today's students resemble savvy consumers who value convenience and quick feedback over the educational quality of their courses.

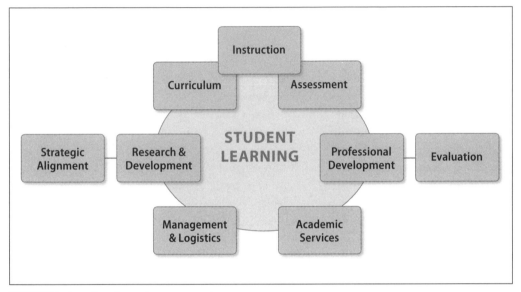

FIGURE I.2 ▶ e-Learning system components

To establish effective online and hybrid programs, educators must view e-learning as part of a larger system that consists of a set of functional components that must all work together to achieve a common goal. Figure I.2 depicts nine functional components of an e-learning system that must work together to facilitate student achievement (Hirumi, 2000, 2010). Figure I.2 also highlights the focus areas of this book series: *instruction designed to facilitate achievement of specified outcomes,* along with two closely interrelated components—*curriculum* and *assessment.*

The nine functional components of an e-learning system are the following: (1) strategic alignment, which aligns the mission and plans of the e-learning system with the mission and plans of the larger educational institution, organization, or system; (2) research and development, which facilitate the integration as well as the dissemination of new knowledge and information generated outside and within the system; (3) curriculum, which specifies and organizes learning outcomes; (4) instruction, which involves the deliberate arrangement of events, including tools and techniques, for facilitating achievement of specified learning outcomes; (5) assessment, which defines the methods and criteria for determining whether students have achieved the curriculum's outcomes; (6) management and logistics, which bring together the human and physical resources necessary to support the system, including strategic plans, policies, procedures, and budgets; (7) academic services, which cover a wide range of support for students, such as (but not limited to) admissions, registration, fee payment, financial aid, academic advising, and so on; (8) professional development, which ensures that all system stakeholders have the skills and knowledge necessary to fulfill their roles and responsibilities; and (9) evaluation, which serves to improve the effectiveness and efficiency of all the system's components. Addressing each system component in detail is well beyond the scope of this book series. Rather, the three books focus on the instructional components of the system, covering different instructional strategies, tools, and techniques for facilitating e-learning, which, in turn, necessitate some discussion of curriculum and assessment.

Taken together, the three books in this series have been written to provide valuable insights for educators and instructional designers tasked with designing online and hybrid e-learning environments. I based the plans for each book's chapters on more than 15 years of experience designing and developing my own online and hybrid courses, as well as helping others in K–12 and higher education, and in business and industry across North America, South America, and the Middle East to establish and improve e-learning programs. The books' chapters are also based on the skills, knowledge, and insights of my colleagues who have also experienced many years of teaching and learning online. If you think that a systematic and systemic approach to e-learning, grounded in research and theory, may help you in your efforts to create high-quality online and hybrid courses, I encourage you to use this book to design rich, engaging, and memorable learning experiences for your students. In addition, if you do use one of the strategies included in this book, or if you know of and use other strategies grounded in research and theory to design an online or hybrid learning environment, please let me know; I'd love to hear from you. The more we can bring grounded practice and systematic design to light, the more I think we can do to increase the quality of e-learning environments and improve education for our students.

References

Allen, M. (2012). *Leaving ADDIE for SAM: An agile model for developing the best learning experiences.* Alexandria, VA: ASTD Press.

Dick, W., Carey, L., & Carey, J. O. (2009). *The systematic design of instruction* (7th ed.). Upper Saddle River, NJ: Pearson.

Hannafin, M., Hannafin, K., & Land, S. (1997). Grounded practice and the design of constructivist learning environments. *Educational Technology Research and Development, 45*(2), 101–117.

Hirumi, A. (2000). Chronicling the challenges of web-basing a degree program: A systems perspective. *The Quarterly Review of Distance Education, 1*(2), 89–108.

Hirumi, A. (2010). *21st century e-learning systems: The need for systemic thinking and change.* Keynote presentation at the 2nd Annual International Conference on e-Learning and Teaching, hosted by the Iran University for Science and Technology, Tehran, Iran, November 30–December 2.

Smith, P. L., & Ragan, T. J. (1999). *Instructional design* (2nd ed.). Upper Saddle River, NJ: Prentice-Hall.

CHAPTER 1

Managing Large Online Courses
Pedagogical Approaches
and Technological Tools

Richard Hartshorne

Online learning is growing rapidly across the United States, as more and more students and educators become familiar with the benefits of learning unconstrained by time and place.

J. F. Watson, A National Primer on K–12 Online Learning, 2007, p. 2

WITH SHRINKING BUDGETS, advances in technology, rising school enrollments, teacher attrition, and the growing extracurricular demands on K–12 students, the current expansion of online learning at the K–12 level is expected to escalate over the next decade. Many states have recognized the potential benefits of online teaching and learning to address issues such as decreasing budgets, equity, and access and have begun integrating online learning into the K–12 curriculum. With these increases, it is essential that states and school districts develop innovative solutions to address the growing demand. Sound pedagogical approaches and the use of both traditional and emerging technological tools allow for numerous approaches to increasing the effectiveness and efficiency of large, K–12 online courses. In this chapter, an overview of the current state of online learning in K–12 settings will be provided. Following this, a snapshot of what an effective K–12 online teaching and learning environment looks like will be shown.

The chapter will then transition into a discussion of methods of using pedagogical approaches and traditional and emerging technological tools to support the management of large, K–12 online courses. The discussion for each of the pedagogical approaches will include an introduction to the approach in K–12 online learning environments, benefits and drawbacks to consider when implementing the approach in large online courses, and specific examples of the implementation of the approach in a large online course. Similar to the pedagogical approaches addressed previously, the discussion of each of the technological tools will include an introduction to the technological application in K–12 online learning environments, issues related to the implementation of the technological tools in K–12 online learning environments, and specific examples of uses of the technological applications in large online courses.

Educators are realizing the benefits of online teaching and learning. Because the learning environment is online, geographically dispersed students can access courses as long as they have Internet connectivity and a requisite collection of hardware and software. With online access, students and schools can save time and money by eliminating or reducing the cost of commuting and reducing other costs associated with brick-and-mortar schools. Students can also complete many online activities at their own pace and complete assignments at their convenience, which has a number of pedagogical advantages. Teachers can also individualize instruction, as well as assign online remediation and enrichment activities, to improve students' performances and increase their satisfaction.

With the benefits of online teaching and learning, coupled with shrinking budgets, rising school enrollments, and teacher attrition, it is expected that the current expansion of online learning at the K–12 level will continue to escalate over the next decade (Allen & Seaman, 2011). However, to meet the growing demand and realize cost savings, administrators are filling online courses with large numbers of students; it is not unusual for some courses to have more than one hundred students. Such increases require instructors to develop innovative solutions to manage and otherwise facilitate online learning.

In this chapter, I identify and discuss pedagogical approaches and technological tools that you may use to manage large online courses. I begin to discuss pedagogical approaches by defining each method and identifying similar techniques. I then describe the benefits and drawbacks of implementing each approach and provide specific examples of how each approach may be applied to help manage a large online course. I then switch my focus to traditional and emerging technological tools that you may use to help manage large online courses. My discussion of tools begins with an introduction to how each technology is applied in K–12 online learning environments, followed by implementation issues, and finally, specific examples of how each tool may be applied to help manage large online courses.

Pedagogical Approaches Supporting the Management of K–12 Online Courses

Sound pedagogical approaches can increase the effectiveness and efficiency of learning in large, online K–12 courses. In this section, I focus on collaboration, peer assessments and self-reviews, chunking content and communications, formal and informal assessments, and online discussion forums.

Collaboration

Collaboration in large online courses may be a useful pedagogical approach for reducing your workload while offering numerous educational benefits for your students. A collaborative online learning environment might involve students placed in a group to solve a common problem, discuss contemporary issues, brainstorm ideas, and complete a variety of projects. Collaborative activities can provide significant time savings for the instructor by reducing the number of assignments requiring feedback (Hirumi, 2003), while affording students opportunities to develop essential interpersonal communication and teamwork skills (Johnson & Johnson, 1986).

Benefits and Drawbacks. Research studies have espoused the critical role that collaboration plays in online teaching and learning environments, as well as its numerous benefits (Brookfield, 1995; Kearsley, 2000; Palloff & Pratt, 2005; Siemens, 2005). Many benefits of collaborative learning are correlated with benefits of active learning. Affording students with various opportunities to interact with peers, the instructor, course content, and other experts may promote students' critical and creative thinking, decrease social isolation, and develop teamwork skills. Alternatively, addressing the potential drawbacks of collaborative learning environments, such as differences in student abilities, student apathy toward collaborative activities, and a lack of collaborative skills among students, can be cumbersome. While many of these issues are related, it is important that they are all addressed at the onset of collaborative learning environments.

It is important to maximize the benefits of collaborative learning activities while minimizing the drawbacks. For example, to address differences in student abilities, a number of processes can be used for more effective group selection. First, select group sizes that are appropriate to the scope and context of the collaborative activity. Second, clearly outline the various roles of group members. Third, while it may be important to have an element of randomness to group selection, it is also important to ensure that all groups are heterogeneous. Providing a mix of students within each group can allow for multiple perspectives to be addressed within the collaborative environment.

To address student apathy toward collaboration, stress the importance of teamwork in today's workplace, identify its benefits, and note the negative consequences for individuals and groups when one or more members do not participate. For example, the need to cooperate with others, work effectively in teams, communicate with others in a group setting, develop rapport, motivate others, and cope with unexpected challenges are all characteristics of real-world work settings. Next, to address any lack of collaborative skills among students, the instructor's scaffolding of the collaborative activity and environment may be necessary. Begin with simple, low-stakes collaborative activities and transition to more complex, high-stakes collaborative activities. To maximize the benefits of collaboration, clearly define means and methods of group communication, activity objectives, and the roles of participating members within individual groups.

Collaboration Examples. Collaboration plays a central role throughout my large online courses. I incorporate a number of formal and informal, simple and complex, and small-scale and large-scale collaborative activities. One example is the development of a team Internet scavenger hunt. In the Internet scavenger hunt activity, teams of students select a grade level and subject area and must create an Internet scavenger hunt that consists of a series of questions for which the responses can be found on the web.

To initiate rapport, all students contribute to an "Introduce Yourself Forum" by providing a "top ten" list about themselves (Figure 1.1). This activity allows students to get to know each other, at least to some degree.

FIGURE 1.1 ▶ "Introduce Yourself Forum" activity

I then facilitate an exercise called "Create a Team Wiki," in which each group creates an initial wiki (Figure 1.2). Each team determines which wiki host they will use, establishes roles for group members, addresses the color scheme and layout of the initial wiki, and adds all group members as editors of the wiki. This small-scale, relatively low-stakes exercise allows for group members to work together initially, to examine the strengths and weaknesses of team members, and to develop a stronger sense of community within the group. Finally, the students create the group Internet scavenger hunt. While this seemingly involves a great deal of scaffolding for a group activity, the initial work that goes into the development of community enhances the likelihood of more successful future collaborative endeavors and fosters a collaborative environment from the beginning of the course, which is pivotal to the overall success of large online classes.

Create a Team Wiki

You will be using a team wiki for several assignments this term. It's time now to create that team wiki. Follow the directions below:

1. As a team, determine who will be your team leader if you have not already done so.
2. Review
   o Wikispaces - http://www.wikispaces.com/
   o PBWorks - http://pbworks.com/
3. As a team, determine which wiki site you will be using.
4. Each team leader should create the wiki for your team by doing the following:

   • Go to the website and follow the instructions for creating a wiki site
   • Choose the FREE version.
   • Please take time to 'make it your own' - add team member names, change colors, etc.
   • Both wiki sites offer great instructions for getting started.

5. The team leader should invite all team members and me to the wiki space.
6. Submit the URL (web address) of your team wiki here.
7. **Other than changing the look of your wiki, you are not required to complete any assignment this week.**

Wikis are very popular in schools with both students and teachers. They allow someone to publish on the web with little technical knowledge and to work collaboratively with other teachers and/or students. Hopefully, some of your assignments/activities will allow you to see how wikis can be used with students.

FIGURE 1.2 ▶ Instructions for "Create a Team Wiki" exercise

Informal and Formal Assessments

Formal assessments, such as exams and structured course projects, provide clear means of determining student knowledge, skills, and dispositions, as well as documenting student achievement. Informal assessments, such as quizzes, presentations, and discussion forums, while measuring student performance, serve as indicators of student growth and understanding of course materials and processes. Using a mix of formal and informal assessments can reduce your workload as well as improve the effectiveness of large online courses.

Benefits and Drawbacks. Formal assessments are great tools for sorting and ranking students. Such arranging, via grades or other means, allows for more individualized instruction that may improve the structure of your online class. Formal assessments provide students and parents with information and structured feedback about student performance that is necessary to remediate or enrich instruction and ensure students meet and, if possible, go beyond expectations. However, formal assessments can increase your workload. Formal assessments require you to review and evaluate students' assignments or responses on exams, tasks that may readily become overwhelming with a large class of students. Technological advances provide tools that mediate such increases. For example, testing tools within learning management systems often include methods of automatic grading. While essay questions or other open-ended items typically require manual grading and can be time-consuming, the reduced time in grading from automation can be a significant timesaver.

Informal assessments can be integrated into a large online course by asking questions during informal asynchronous discussion forums and synchronous course meetings (i.e., web conferences), as well as in games, journals, blog posts, or other structured or unstructured activities. Informal assessments might also include measures of sub-steps or scaffolding activities as part of the journey toward completing a larger, formal course assignment. Informal assessments are low-stress, low-stakes methods of determining the progress of and providing feedback to students at various phases in the learning process. They also provide students with a variety of instructional formats, increasing the likelihood of improved performance. Informal assessments, in conjunction with formal assessments, are excellent tools for getting a comprehensive view of a student's knowledge, skills, and dispositions.

However, while some informal assessments may decrease teachers' workloads, others may not. Thus, when integrating informal assessments into large online courses, it is important to consider their influence on teachers' workloads, their pedagogical benefits, and a few additional implementation issues. In large online courses, more time-consuming informal assessments include student writing samples and manually graded diagnostic assessments. Integrating these into large online courses is impractical. However, less time-consuming assessments, such as online discussions, group projects, and automatically scored diagnostic measures, can reduce teachers' workloads while providing large amounts of data about students' progress and performance.

Informal and Formal Assessment Examples. In large (or small) online courses, keep in mind that not everything has to be graded. With a large number of students and a robust curriculum, grading all activities is impractical and not pedagogically sound. Thus, it is important to combine formal and informal assessments appropriately. One way to combine formal and informal assessments is through the use of diagnostic assessments. Figure 1.3 illustrates three items from a diagnostic instrument used for an introductory course on technology in education. The "Focus Area" item allows me to customize feedback and provide a more individualized learning experience. The "Online Classes" item provides experiential information related to each student, which allows me to provide additional guidance and scaffolding for those with limited experience as online learners. Following these forum activities are a series of more specific items related to tools in online courses. The "Online Discussions" item, illustrated in Figure 1.3, is one such example. Other aspects of the diagnostic instrument relate to technological access and experience with various technological applications.

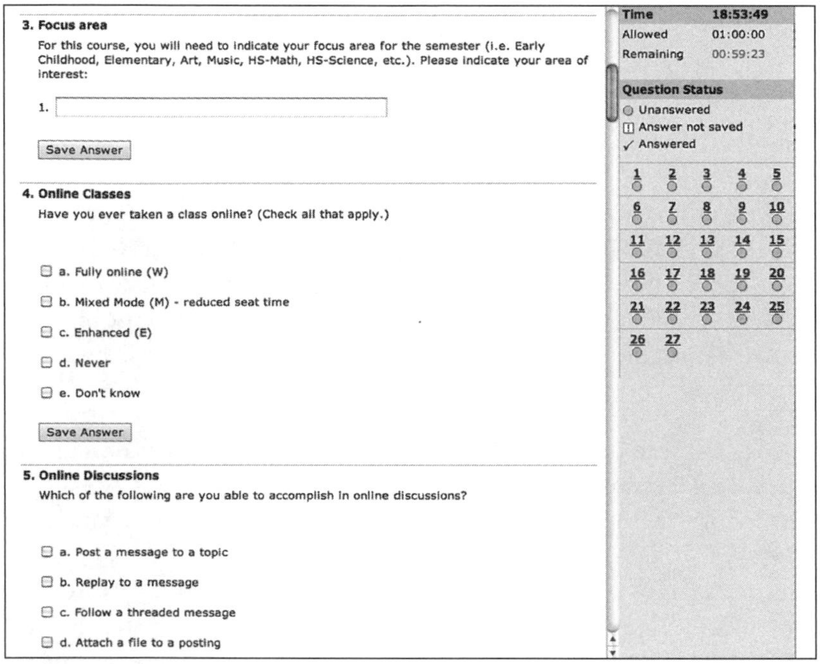

3. Focus area

For this course, you will need to indicate your focus area for the semester (i.e. Early Childhood, Elementary, Art, Music, HS-Math, HS-Science, etc.). Please indicate your area of interest:

1.

Save Answer

4. Online Classes

Have you ever taken a class online? (Check all that apply.)

- a. Fully online (W)
- b. Mixed Mode (M) - reduced seat time
- c. Enhanced (E)
- d. Never
- e. Don't know

Save Answer

5. Online Discussions

Which of the following are you able to accomplish in online discussions?

- a. Post a message to a topic
- b. Replay to a message
- c. Follow a threaded message
- d. Attach a file to a posting

Time	18:53:49
Allowed	01:00:00
Remaining	00:59:23

Question Status

Unanswered
Answer not saved
✓ Answered

1 2 3 4 5
6 7 8 9 10
11 12 13 14 15
16 17 18 19 20
21 22 23 24 25
26 27

FIGURE 1.3 ▶ Snapshot of introductory diagnostic assessment items

Peer and Self-Assessments

Peer and self-assessments are particular types of formal or informal assessments that you may use to enhance learning while reducing your workload in large online courses. Peer assessment occurs when one student provides some judgment or assessment of the work of a peer. Peer assessment might involve students in the same group assessing the quality of their peers' contributions to a collaborative assignment, judging the role of a student's performance in a collaborative activity, or even assessing or judging individual students' assignments. Alternatively, self-assessment involves a student reflecting upon and assessing his or her own work or his or her contributions and participation in a collaborative activity. While these can often be time-consuming to develop, such activities can provide significant time savings for instructors, and they can provide students with opportunities for exploration of the fundamentals of the assessment process, including various types of evaluation.

Benefits and Drawbacks. Collaborative activities can be more beneficial if students are involved in the assessment process. Peer reviews and self-assessments can increase students' responsibility, enhance students' critical thinking skills, develop students' assessment skills, allow for a more thorough interaction with the course content and activities, and provide a more engaging learning environment for students. Activities that support peer assessments include students' development of assessment criteria and the inclusion of a detailed peer-assessment instrument or self-assessment protocols that facilitate students' abilities to (a) work well with other group members, (b) complete tasks on time, (c) provide feedback on work of other group members, and (d) contribute effectively to the group dynamic, among others. Other advantages of peer and self-assessments include increased student ownership over their learning, increased development of reflective skills, enhanced clarity of desired outcomes, increased perception of fairness in the assessment process, and more of an insiders' assessment of the contribution of each member of a specific collaborative activity (Black & William, 1998).

While there are numerous advantages to both peer and self-assessments, a number of disadvantages need to be considered. First, while the process can reduce the workload of the instructor, particularly in large online courses, it often takes significant time to prepare students to be effective peer reviewers and self-assessors. Many times, students feel ill-equipped as peer reviewers or self-assessors or are simply reluctant to assess their peers or themselves. Also, issues such as grade inflation due to overrating peers or lack of differentiation in ratings must be considered. Social issues, such as altered ratings of friends or students with personal issues, or feelings of resentment toward having to do work a student might view as the role of the instructor are also common. Additionally, determining an appropriate weight for self- and peer-assessment activities can sometimes be difficult. When instructors implement peer and self-assessments, as with other pedagogical approaches, they must weigh the advantages and disadvantages against each other, as well as ensure that the assessments meet the course's instructional goals.

Peer and Self-Assessment Examples. To reduce instructors' workloads and address students' feelings of isolation in large online courses, collaborative group activities are often utilized. Consequently, such courses provide great venues for peer and self-assessments in collaborative activities. When developing a peer and self-assessment for collaborative group activities, it is important to consider a variety of perspectives. For example, in a group setting, members have a number of non-product-related roles, such as completing assigned tasks in a timely manner, getting along with teammates, providing appropriate and timely feedback, and sharing information with group members. Peer assessments also have product/activity-related components, such as the quality of individual input on final products. It is important to determine an appropriate balance in both the non-product and product-related aspects of peer assessments.

Figures 1.4–1.6 illustrate peer/self-assessment instruments I use for large-scale collaborative projects in a number of my courses. Figure 1.4 illustrates the context of the assignment and the importance of providing useful and relevant assessments of peer work and self contributions. Figures 1.5 and 1.6 illustrate what the peer/self-assessment tools look like. As you can see in the these figures, the focus of the instrument is on participation and contribution related to different aspects of a collaborative project (e.g., attendance at meetings, meeting deadlines, providing feedback to group members, and contributing one's fair share). When implementing peer and self-assessments, it is important to provide guidance for each area of assessment, as well as to make clear distinctions between levels of performance, and to give opportunities for students to provide detailed feedback regarding assessment decisions. Though this guidance may take a bit of additional time, affording students opportunities to assess themselves and others in collaborative projects is pedagogically beneficial, and it reduces the instructor's workload.

Update this Assignment
View 5 submitted assignments

As you know, you and your colleagues are currently working on a group instructional development project for the EIST 6140 course. Individual participation and contribution to the group project is essential to ensure that all members of the group have an opportunity to learn from the project. Each group member is being asked to complete an evaluation form on their own participation as a self-assessment. In addition, each group member is being asked to complete a peer evaluation form for each member of the group. When returned, the form data will be used to generate individual scores. Your report will include your self-evaluation and the combined results of the other peer evaluation forms. Individual peer responses will not be associated with the particular respondent but will be reported as an aggregate assessment with instructor feedback/comments. So please provide candid and constructive feedback about what each of your peers can do to increase the value of the project and your opportunities for learning.

EIST 6140 Peer Evaluation 1 Form
To submit the document, re-save the form in the following formats: yourname-peer-eval-personevaluated.docx. So if I was doing a self-evaluation, the filename would be hartshorne-peer-eval-hartshorne.docx. Submit the files to the course system by browsing and submitting using the button below.

Due date: Sunday, 13 February 2011, 11:55 PM

Submission draft

No files submitted yet

Upload a file (Max size: 5MB)

Browse...

Upload this file

Notes

No entry

Edit

Final submission for assignment marking

Send for marking

Moodle Docs for this page

FIGURE 1.4 ▶ Introductory text for a peer/self-assessment activity

Peer Evaluation Form

Instructions:

You and your colleagues are currently working on a group project for this course. Individual participation and contribution to the group project is essential to ensure that all members of the group have an opportunity to learn from the project. Each group member is being asked to complete an evaluation form on their own participation as a self-assessment. In addition, each group member is being asked to complete a peer evaluation form for each member of the group. When returned, the form data will be used to generate individual scores. Your report will include your self evaluation and the combined results of the other peer evaluation forms. Individual peer responses will not be associated with the particular respondent but will be reported as an aggregate assessment. So, please provide candid and constructive feedback about what each of your peers can do to increase the value of the project and your opportunities for learning.

Peer Information:

Please answer each of the following items.

(1) Individual being evaluated:
☐Student 1 ☐Student 2 ☐Student 3 ☐Student 4 ☐Student 5

(2) Your relationship to the person being evaluated: ☐Self ☐Colleague

(Ctrl)

Participation and Contribution:

Considering your experiences of the person being evaluated during this group project, indicate how strongly you "agree" or "disagree" with each statement.

This individual....	Strongly Agree	Agree	Neutral	Disagree	Strongly Disagree
(3) Attends project team meetings.	☐	☐	☐	☐	☐
(4) Productively participates at project team meetings.	☐	☐	☐	☐	☐
(5) Contributes their "fair share" to the work effort.	☐	☐	☐	☐	☐
(6) Delivers on commitments / deadlines made to the group.	☐	☐	☐	☐	☐

FIGURE 1.5 ▶ Part 1 of a peer/self-assessment rubric

This individual...	Strongly Agree	Agree	Neutral	Disagree	Strongly Disagree
(7) Stays active in the project by reviewing other members' work.	☐	☐	☐	☐	☐
(8) Provides feedback to other group members on ways to improve their work contributions to the group.	☐	☐	☐	☐	☐
(9) Uses feedback from other group members to improve work contributions to the group.	☐	☐	☐	☐	☐
(10) Ensures that all group members understand the tasks associated with their assigned project role.	☐	☐	☐	☐	☐
(11) Shares lessons learned so that all group members can gain from her experience with the project.	☐	☐	☐	☐	☐
(12) Does whatever is necessary to make the project team successful.	☐	☐	☐	☐	☐
(13) Is a person that I would want to work with again on other projects if the opportunity were to exist.	☐	☐	☐	☐	☐
(14) What other thoughts would you share with this colleague that would enhance the project team's experience and instructional product?					

FIGURE 1.6 ▶ Part 2 of a peer/self-assessment rubric

Chunking Content and Communications

Chunking can be defined as breaking down information into smaller portions to make the content easier to comprehend and assimilate. In a large online classroom, chunking of information is also an excellent strategy for individualizing instruction.

Benefits and Drawbacks. The benefits of chunking information and communications are numerous for large online courses. First, they allow students to organize and access course information more efficiently and effectively. Chunking information allows you to present online content in a more manageable, logical, and easy to understand manner. Second, when a consistent process and hierarchy are adopted, chunking can scaffold a variety of course information, including course processes, protocols, content, activities, assessments, and updates. Such chunking is particularly useful from a cognitive perspective, as the students can focus on the course's information rather than its structure. Chunking instructor-student communications can also help students keep up with course events. Third, while typically associated with linear instruction, chunking can also be applied to complex, nonlinear content, as it is particularly effective when stressing the associations between and among related concepts.

However, due to the repetitive nature of chunking, students can often overlook important information or processes. Thus, it is important to maintain a chunking method that is consistent and organized in a logical manner, with smaller, simpler chunks transitioning to larger, more complex chunks later in the course.

Chunking Content and Communication Examples. One effective technique for managing large online courses is to provide small chunks of communication to all students in brief, very regular intervals in multiple formats. For example, in a number of my large online courses,

I post asynchronous video announcements that provide information on expectations and course processes on a monthly basis as depicted in Figure 1.7. The videos are typically accompanied by audio (podcast) announcements that provide information that might be needed at a more regular interval, perhaps weekly. Information in weekly audio updates might include reminders of important course events and protocols, general feedback about course activities, or information on modifications to the course structure, such as a previously unscheduled help session with students.

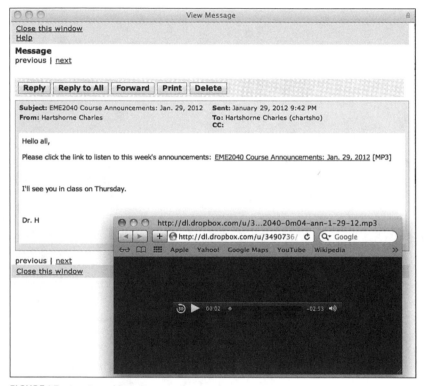

FIGURE 1.7 ▶ A weekly audio announcement

I provide more regular text-based announcements every few days with small bits of information designed to facilitate instructor-student communications as illustrated in Figure 1.8. With each form of communication, it is also important to provide a certain level of redundancy to ensure that students do not overlook important information.

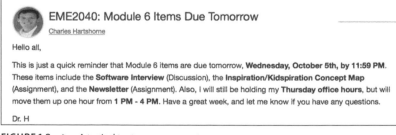

FIGURE 1.8 ▶ A typical text announcement

Discussion Forums

Many learning theorists believe that learning is a social process and occurs through learners' interactions and exchanges of information among each other (e.g., Bruner, 1996; Lave & Wenger, 1991; Vygotsky, 1978). Many also cite active participation as a critical component of learning (Ferdig, 2007). Discussion forums support such beliefs as well as facilitate approaches previously mentioned in the chapter (i.e., informal assessments, collaborative work, peer assessment, asynchronous interactions). When implemented appropriately, discussion forums can be very useful tools for managing large, K–12 online courses.

Discussion forums are web-based entities that allow for asynchronous interactions among stakeholders in the learning environment. Embedded as a component of many learning management systems, discussion forums allow for students to reflect on a prompt, provide a meaningful response to the prompt, and then provide thoughtful insights and multiple perspectives in response to peers' postings. As learning management systems adapt over time, applications of the "discussion forum" entity will continue to improve. For example, Moodle, a popular open source learning management system, includes a number of variations on the traditional "discussion forum" that can be embedded into the teaching and learning environment. There is a "single thread" discussion, in which a prompt or question is posted, and all participants respond in a single thread, rather than all creating their own individual threads (and associated replies). There is also a Q&A forum, in which specific users are not allowed to access/read the content of other posts until they have written an original post. Other discussion forum types in Moodle include a News forum, in which an instructor can post important course announcements, but the students do not have the ability to respond, as well as the traditional multi-thread discussion forum, which allows course participants to create new threads and reply to other participants' threads. Each of the discussion forum types possesses varying pedagogical benefits in the large online classroom.

Benefits and Drawbacks. Research cites numerous benefits and limitations of using discussion forums in large online teaching and learning environments. Among the benefits is the development of community among students, reduced instructor time responding to student questions (chunking communications), and more regular participation by a larger representation of the class than in traditional face-to-face courses. Discussion forums also allow for students' reflections, promote critical thinking, increase the time students are engaged with course materials, afford flexibility in the learning environment, and facilitate the presentation of multiple perspectives.

Many drawbacks associated with discussion forums are related to the asynchronous nature of the interactions. For example, discussion forums are typically much more useful for large groups than for smaller groups. With smaller groups, it can be more difficult to elicit detailed, meaningful discussion posts. However, it is important not to make the large groups too large, as the number of posts and replies can be overwhelming, resulting in important information being overlooked. While discussion forums are useful in developing community, it is important to integrate other social interactions in large online courses.

Discussion Forum Examples. It is critical to develop a sense of community among students in large online courses as well as rapport with and among students. To do this in my large online courses, I utilize an "Introduce Yourself" asynchronous discussion forum as depicted in Figure 1.1. In this forum, students list "Top Ten Things" about themselves and then reply to a number of their peers' postings. Additionally, to facilitate interaction between groups in a large course, I also establish a series of discussion forums specifically for interaction among group members (Figure 1.9). Groups use such informal forums to communicate with each other on collaborative activities throughout a course.

FIGURE 1.9 ▶ Individualized team discussion forums

If there is a need to review content from a particular course activity, you may want to use a synchronous videoconference. Because a single session might not be practical for large courses, I typically provide a series of alternative days and times for synchronous sessions. Additionally, I record and archive all synchronous sessions (chunking communications) for those who were unable to attend or for future review by those who attended.

There are also a number of other potential applications of discussion forums to manage large, online K–12 courses. First, as a tool to decrease instructors' workloads in large online courses, I often use a one-way discussion forum to chunk communications and provide guidance in large online courses. For example, Figure 1.10 illustrates a series of course announcements for a semester-long course.

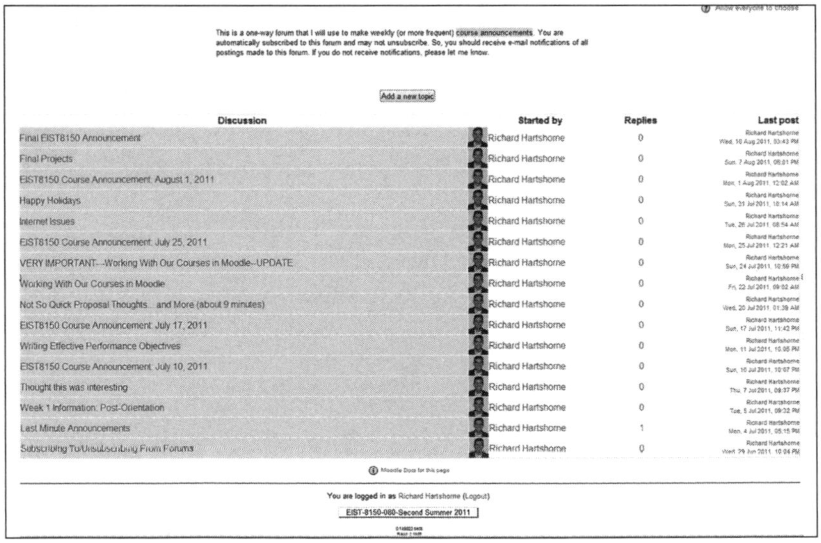

FIGURE 1.10 ▶ A "Course Announcements" one-way discussion forum

You will notice that there are no replies and the announcements are spread out somewhat regularly throughout the semester. The lack of a facility for students to reply is useful in this case because it reduces the anxiety of having to participate in all forums. If students have questions related to the content of an announcement, they can follow up with the instructor on an individual basis.

Other examples of online discussion forums are group debates, critiques, and explorations. In such forums, a topic or item is presented as a prompt. You can then have groups debate the topic, provide a critique of something associated with the topic, such as a web resource or video, or explore the topic and reply to questions posted to the forum. Students can provide additional resources to support their views that may then be shared with students in subsequent sessions of the course. Using discussion forums in such a manner increases students' accessibility to external content related to the course, promotes collaboration, facilitates the development of community, increases motivation, and promotes social interactions—all benefits of online learning.

Technological Applications to Support Managing Large Online Courses

Learning management systems, wikis, presentation sharing, file sharing, and Voice-over-Internet-Protocol/web conferencing tools are some examples of traditional and emerging technological applications that can play pivotal roles in the management of large, online K–12 courses. These technological applications offer you and your students a variety of technological advances and functionality, such as more immersive and interactive environments, sophisticated and flexible communicative tools, continual access to course content, and ease of organization and dissemination of information (Madden & Fox, 2006; Maloncy, 2007). Such applications have influenced the way K–12 instructors and students create, use, share, and distribute content, as well as the way the content is shared among stakeholders in the educational environment, all much more efficiently than was possible in the past (Dearstyne, 2007).

Many tools, while not specifically designed for use in K–12 teaching and learning environments, possess characteristics that make them ideal for use in large, online K–12 courses. Beneficial characteristics include support for active learning; venues for student-student, student-instructor, and student-content interactions; and opportunities to scaffold learning, all of which are features of effective learning environments (Bruner, 1996; Boulos & Wheelert, 2007; Ferdig, 2007; Johnson & Johnson, 1986; Lave & Wenger, 1991; Sturm, Kennel, McBride, & Kelly, 2008; Vygotsky, 1978). In the next section, I explore a number of these tools along with implementation issues and methods of maximizing the strengths while minimizing the weaknesses of these tools in facilitating the management of large, online K–12 courses.

Learning Management Systems

Learning management systems (LMSs) for K–12 online teaching and learning are web-based software applications that allow for the publication and implementation of online courses. Fundamental instructional tasks, such as the dissemination of course content, documentation of student performance, submission of student work, communication with stakeholders, and tracking of student performance and interactions, are all features that can be managed within an LMS. While functionality of LMSs varies, many integrate a series of tools for presentation, communication, and assessment. While most LMSs contain a general set of features and possess similar basic functionality, their capacities to customize the teaching and learning environment, based on a core set of common features as well as a series of LMS-specific tools, can provide significantly different learning experiences for students and teachers. For example, most LMSs contain tools for synchronous and asynchronous communications, such as email systems, chat rooms, and discussion forums, while others integrate videoconferencing tools, interactive white-boards, and Voice-over Internet Protocol (VoIP) tools.

LMSs can also host text, hyperlinks, animations, videos, graphics, games, simulations, and others and can organize the course materials in a number of ways (e.g., weekly or modular). LMSs also include tools to develop, implement, and manage assessments, such as exams or quizzes. You can create assessment items directly in the LMS or sometimes import items based on a specific format. You can also automatically or manually score assessments and export grades directly to an online grade book. You can also manage course projects, papers, or other products with LMSs. You can disseminate assignment descriptions and grading criteria to students, provide assessment and feedback, and export assessment information to an integrated grade book.

While LMSs are too numerous to discuss in this chapter, two are common among K–12 schools: Moodle (https://moodle.org), an open-source LMS, and Blackboard (www.blackboard.com). Moodle (Figure 1.11) is popular because of its user-friendly student and instructor/developer interface and its constant development of additional functionality from the open-source community. While no direct costs are associated with Moodle, there are costs associated with web hosting, as well as technical support that would be necessary to implement and manage the open-source tool.

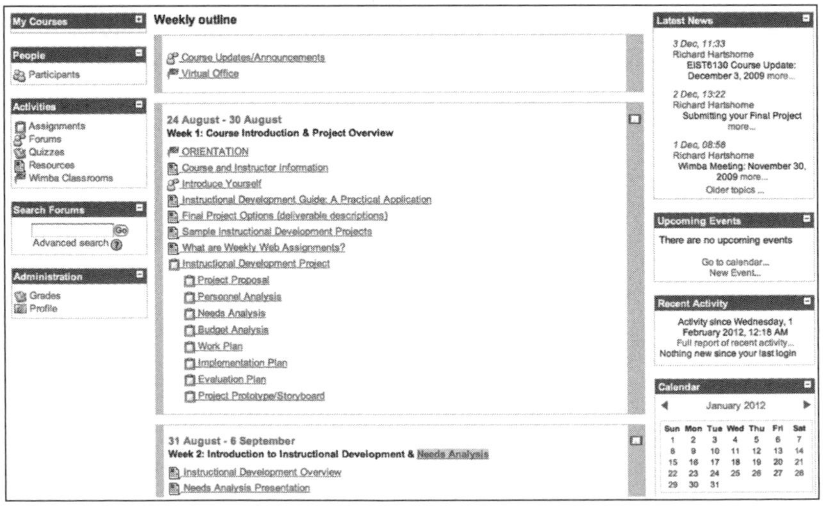

FIGURE 1.11 ▶ Moodle interface and environment

Another common LMS in K–12 online teaching and learning is Blackboard. Blackboard (Figure 1.12) is a commercially available product that provides a variety of LMS-related products to support online teaching and learning. While Blackboard possesses many of the features and functionality of a traditional LMS, it is typically viewed as somewhat difficult to learn, may have limited compatibility with all operating systems, and can be costly (Bradford, Porciello, Balkon, & Backus, 2007). Technical staff fully support Blackboard, which is a major benefit, and its collaboration platform is designed for educators' use. It is not necessary for a school district to allocate significant resources for the implementation and management of Blackboard.

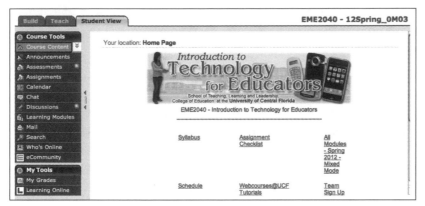

FIGURE 1.12 ▶ The Blackboard environment

Implementation Issues. Though you may not be in a position to select the LMS used by your school district, you should consider a number of implementation issues related to the functionality of LMSs. If you are a savvy tech user, your school's technology coordinator or principal may well ask you for your input on the decision. As previously mentioned, functionality varies among LMSs, not all of which are useful in managing large, online K–12 courses. Thus, it is critical that you explore the features of any LMSs being considered or the LMS already utilized by your school district to determine which features are appropriate for your audience of students and the courses you teach, based on your instructional strategy (as delineated in Hirumi's Chapter 2, Applying Grounded Strategies to Design and Sequence e-Learning Interactions, of the first book in this series, *Online and Hybrid Learning Design Fundamentals*). It is also important to consider the phases or units of each course in which particular LMS features will be utilized. For example, features might be limited to assignments and discussion forums early in a course, followed by text chats as the course progresses, and then videoconferencing later in the course. Essentially, with users that are new either to online learning or the specific LMS platform you're using, implementing too many features too early can be overwhelming. Thus, it is important to scaffold the features and functionality of the learning management system utilized in your course. It is also important that you stay current with various features and updates supplied by the LMS, as these new tools potentially allow for more robust online K–12 teaching and learning, including how they may help you manage large, online K–12 courses effectively.

LMS Examples. LMSs offer educators and students a number of benefits. One of the major yet often overlooked benefits of LMSs is that they provide a centralized learning environment. Using internal LMS tools can be more efficient than using external tools with similar functions. For example, in a number of my courses I use wikis as tools to facilitate collaboration. Even though many external wiki hosts, such as Wikispaces or PBWorks, are readily available and sometimes function in ways superior to Moodle's, I like to use the wiki tool embedded in Moodle because it is easier for my students and me to access. When we use Moodle's wiki tool, we do not have to access an external resource. Sometimes students can become overwhelmed by having to access course information from multiple locations. By using Moodle's embedded wiki tool, I do not have to access numerous external wikis, and students' contributions to the wikis are tracked within the LMS. These conveniences allow me to manage large online courses more effectively and efficiently. As I do not have to spend a lot of time helping students locate my courses' information, activities, and resources, I can spend more time developing subject matter content and providing high-quality feedback to students.

A second way that I use LMSs is to track individual students' activities within a course (e.g., interactions with peers and the instructor and viewings of content), as well as their performances in the course. For example, using the assessment tools within LMSs, I often conduct item analyses, determining which items students mastered and which ones they struggled with. I then alter future instructional activities to produce a different instructional approach or provide remediation/enrichment resources associated with a specific course goal. These analyses are particularly useful when I teach subsequent iterations of large courses, because I spend less time reteaching material and less time tutoring and scaffolding struggling students.

Wikis

Wikis refer to collaborative websites that allow users to interact by adding, removing, or editing site content. Teachers cite wikis, such as Wikipedia, Wikispaces (www.wikispaces.com), PBWorks (http://pbworks.com), and Weebly (www.weebly.com) as effective instructional tools (Ajjan & Hartshorne, 2008; Peterson, 2009) for supporting individualized and social learning and promoting collaboration through group design, development, editing, and peer review (Alexander, 2006).

Implementation Issues. While there are numerous wiki hosts available, most of them have similar features, including the capability to create new pages, edit pages, add users, control the permissions of users, insert various forms of media, track edits and contributors, and others. With wikis, issues associated with collaborative work (mentioned earlier in this chapter under Pedagogical Approaches Supporting the Management of K–12 Courses with the subheading Collaboration), the technological experience of the students, and the use of external wiki versus internal wiki are all factors that must be examined prior to use for online teaching and learning.

Wiki Examples. There are numerous applications of wikis in teaching and learning environments, many of which can be applied to large online courses. First, students within a class can create a single course wiki to host a variety of important information. Information might include class announcements, example work, remediation resources, enrichment resources, or additional material that might be useful to the students.

Many LMSs have embedded wikis (as discussed along with Moodle). Figure 1.13 illustrates a wiki I have utilized in past courses to facilitate communication within the Moodle environment. Once the wiki was created, students could view the wiki from the "View" tab at the top of Figure 1.13, add text, hyperlinks, images, and other content using the "Edit" tab, view pages linked to the wiki from the "Links" tab, and see all edits and contributors by viewing the "History" tab. Such features are typical of the other wikis as well.

FIGURE 1.13   ▶   Wiki feature within Moodle

You can oversee students who may be given the responsibility of maintaining a class wiki, thus reducing your workload in large online courses. You can also use it as a tool to provide constant access to course resources and chunk information to share information with parents. Additionally, the course wiki could house individual student wikis. Individual student wikis might include links to various course projects or other products created by students in the course. One example that encompasses a number of the applications discussed is Mrs. Ibrahim's class wiki (http://mrsibrahim.wikispaces.com/home). Other examples can be viewed at Wikispaces' Educational Wikis page (http://educationalwikis.wikispaces.com/Examples+of+educational+wikis).

Podcasting

A podcast is a digital media file, typically in the form of audio or video, that is presented in a series and distributed through a variety of means, usually through subscriptions via really simple syndication (RSS) feeds. Podcasts can be extremely useful in the online teaching and learning environments from both teachers' and students' perspectives. As this is the primary topic of another chapter, I only mention them here as another technological tool for helping manage large online courses and refer interested readers to Curry's Chapter 2, Podcasting in Education: Practices and Precautions, the next chapter in this book.

Presentation Sharing Tools

Social software tools allow users to share various forms of content with family, friends, and other colleagues; they are ubiquitous and popular with K–12 students today (Lenhart & Madden, 2007). Currently, most K–12 students use social networking sites to keep in touch and share information with friends and family and to make new friends. Extending such ideas to educational settings, particularly online settings, can be effective in establishing academic connections, as well as in fostering communication and cooperation within and among classrooms. Presentation sharing tools, such as SlideShare and authorSTREAM, are forms of social software that allow users to share presentations with the entire world or with only a selected group of individuals. Users can also create channels or collections of presentations and assign keywords for ease of searching.

Additionally, viewers can comment on presentations, download presentations, and interact in other ways.

Implementation Issues. As with LMSs, there are numerous presentation sharing tools to consider with various features and functionality. Two of the more common presentation sharing tools are SlideShare (www.slideshare.net), a free online site that allows for sharing PowerPoint presentations, and authorSTREAM (www.authorstream.com), a free online tool that allows sharing narrated PowerPoint presentations. Both of these are cloud-based Web 2.0 tools that provide a great deal of functionality. For example, SlideShare could be billed as the YouTube of PowerPoint presentations, as users can easily search for presentations on a variety of topics. Although not its primary function, SlideShare (Figure 1.14) allows users to create a channel to host their specific works, sets aside space for others' comments, provides controls for access to content, and has numerous sharing features with other social software applications, such as Facebook, Google+, and Twitter.

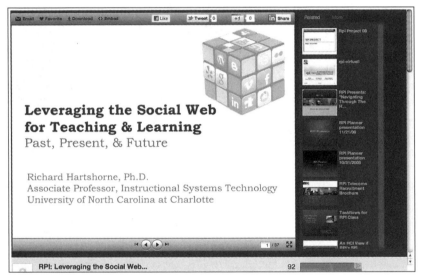

FIGURE 1.14 ▶ The SlideShare interface

AuthorSTREAM (Figure 1.15) is similar to SlideShare with one major difference—the inclusion of audio. Users of authorSTREAM may upload narrated presentations and can convert them to web-based, viewable formats. Both SlideShare and authorSTREAM allow users to follow individual channels or users, which can be quite beneficial in online course environments. Some other presentation sharing tools include SlideRocket (www.sliderocket.com), which is similar in functionality to SlideShare, and VoiceThread (http://voicethread.com), which allows for development of collaborative multimedia slide shows by hosting original content and allotting space for other users to comment via a variety of media (audio, video, or text). Additional tools can be found at Web 2.0: Cool Tools for School (http://cooltoolsforschools.wikispaces.com/Presentation+Tools).

In addition to comparing functionality, further factors need to be considered in selecting an appropriate presentation sharing tool for your course. First, it is important to consider usability, as ease of use for the instructor and students is critical. Second is cost. While all the tools mentioned have free versions; additional features and functionality are available at some cost. Third, consider sustainability. Research the number of users and read reviews of the tool. Because sustainability is not guaranteed, be sure to back up your work and rely on a specific tool minimally. In addition, consider the current and future purposes of the tool. Though you may start out only wanting to share text-based presentations, at a later date you might want to share narrated presentations so it's practical to plan accordingly.

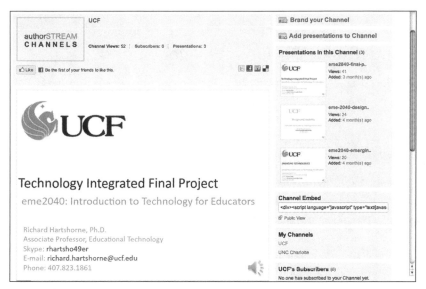

FIGURE 1.15   ▶   Example of authorSTREAM channel

Presentation Sharing Examples. From students' and teachers' perspectives, presentation sharing tools can be implemented in numerous ways in large online classrooms. I often use presentation sharing tools to chunk both course content and communications, as well as to provide guidance on course assignments and activities. In a large online course I was teaching, I saw students having problems grasping the requirements for the final course project. Rather than trying to respond to each email with questions about the project, I created a narrated presentation that gave a detailed walk-through of the project. I then hosted the presentation on authorSTREAM and informed students about its availability via our LMS email system.

Presentation sharing tools may be used to disseminate course management information to students and to allow students to illustrate their knowledge of course content. Essentially, such tools can be used in many of the same ways as podcasts; they also provide additional functionality and the integration of more varied types of media. I often have students create presentations (similar to podcasts) on course content, and these tools promote collaboration, reduce my workload, and allow students a place to publish their work. In past courses, I have created channels or collections of these presentations of student work for others to view. Facilitating assignments that demonstrate students' ability to apply knowledge is always a challenge in large classes. In fact, many large conventional and online classes tend to focus on the transmission of information and the students' ability to recall (rather than apply) knowledge because of the daunting numbers of students per class. By creating channels or collections, I can then use the presentation sharing tool to help my students to organize and access numerous presentations that may result from a large class.

Presentation sharing tools can be used in many other ways: to record podcasts by guest speakers, to review important content, to enrich content with additional multimedia materials, and to create templates for or examples of student work. All of these products could be hosted on a classroom website, a blog, or on a social network group for a particular course to facilitate students' learning and to maintain instructors' workloads at reasonable levels in large online classes.

File Storage/Sharing (Online Document Management)

File storage/sharing sites allow users to store, describe, and share numerous files with others, typically not limiting file type. While these sites can be useful in supporting collaboration among students, they are primarily beneficial as a management tool for online instructors. While not specifically designed for education applications, file storage/sharing tools offer features that make them useful for managing large online classrooms.

Implementation Issues. If you choose to use file storage/sharing tools to help manage large online courses, you need to consider a number of implementation issues. First, for legal reasons, for example, the Family Educational Rights and Privacy Act (FERPA) of 1974, it is important that student information not be stored on file storage sites. Due to insufficient control over some sites' security, it is conceivable that individuals who should not have access to student data could access it. Second, while most of the file storage/sharing sites have web browser-based access, many of them have web browser plug-ins that simplify the storage and sharing processes. However, within school districts, plug-ins often are not allowed. Thus, it is important to understand your school district's Acceptable Use Policy. As with other tools addressed in this chapter, it is also important to consider ease of use for you and your students; cost for advanced features, if needed; sustainability; and the present and future purposes of using the tool. As time lapses, so might the functionality of either file storage/sharing tools, or other tools mentioned in the chapter might integrate their file storage/sharing features, eliminating the need to use a separate program in your online course.

Some of the more popular file storage/sharing tools include Dropbox (www.dropbox.com), which provides at least 2 GB of free storage and more for educators; Cloud Drive (www.driveoncloud.com), which provides up to 5 GB of free storage; and Box (www.box.com), which offers up to 5 GB of free storage. Also, Google Cloud Storage (https://developers.google.com/storage), allows for 1 GB of free storage but may also be integrated with other Google tools, such as Gmail or Google Apps.

File Storage/Sharing Examples. There are numerous ways you can implement file storage/sharing tools to facilitate large online classes. For example, I use file storage/sharing tools to host student work samples and share past work with students in subsequent semesters. I also archive useful tutorials and other resources that proved to be valuable teaching tools for individualizing instruction and remediating students.

In addition to archiving information, you can also use many file sharing tools as a makeshift web host. For example, I've uploaded HTML (web) files to sites such as Dropbox, placed them in a public folder, and shared the URL with students. The content would then appear as a typical web page. Due to the potential to host very large files and varying file types, using file sharing/ storage tools might also provide more flexibility than some "for cost" web hosting services. In a less formal manner, I have also used file storage/sharing tools to disseminate large files that could not be disseminated using other methods, such as email or through an LMS, which both typically have file size limitations. File storage/sharing tools also allow students to submit assignments and other materials to you that may be too large to be submitted via the LMS or email.

Instructors can use file storage/sharing tools to facilitate collaborative work among students. File storage/sharing tools are great for allowing groups of students to post their work and share with others in their group, promoting real-world collaboration and helping students manage collabora- tive projects more easily. Of course, there are other tools to support collaborative learning, but the capability to share large files and minimize file type restrictions affords more flexibility in the collaborative learning environment, which can be particularly useful in large online courses.

Voice-over-Internet Protocol and Web Conferencing Tools

Web conferencing tools, such as Skype, ooVoo, and join.me, use VoIP to facilitate communica- tions and the sharing of information over the Internet. Initially, VoIP tools allowed users to send and receive phone calls over the web to other computers, cell phones, or landlines. More recently, VoIP services have grown to facilitate synchronous meetings and sharing of information in various multimedia formats among groups of individuals in geographically dispersed locations all over the web. For example, Skype users can share files, share their screens, share videos, and participate in group videoconferences.

Web conferencing tools can help you manage large online courses by facilitating synchronous video communications, useful for providing immediate feedback, developing a sense of commu- nity, increasing student motivation, and promoting social learning and development.

Implementation Issues. Synchronous learning opportunities, such as audio and web conferences, include environments in which all participants are present in a learning environment at the same time. Benefits of synchronous learning experiences include immediate feedback (Pan & Sullivan, 2005), community development, increased student motivation, and facilitation of social interac- tion (Im & Lee, 2003/2004). Some drawbacks of synchronous learning opportunities include lack of time flexibility (students often take online courses so they don't have to be at a specific location at a specific time); difficulties in use with large groups of students and in facilitating task-oriented interactions; and some students' lack of devices or skills to fulfill technical requirements. If you choose to use web conferencing tools to facilitate online learning and the management of large online classes, you must consider a number of implementation issues. First, accessibility is impor- tant to consider. When determining which web conferencing tool to use and in what capacity, you must consider where students will use the tool. For example, if students are to web confer- ence via mobile devices, it is important to examine which tools work best with mobile devices, as some might require WiFi connections, while others might work well with typical data plans.

Also, it is important to consider the technological requirements for each tool and how they fit with the typical learner. For example, if the majority of students in a course do not have access to web cams, then it might be useful to select one of the VoIP tools with limited functionality. Next, consider platform dependency. If the web conferencing tool is best utilized only on PC formats but students are also using Macintosh or other platforms, a switch in the VoIP or web conferencing tool might be necessary.

Next, consider costs for students and the educational institution. While most of the tools discussed in this chapter provide a variety of free features, it might be necessary to ask students to upgrade their tech tools, depending on how they need to be used in the course setting. For example, file sharing and screen sharing of some VoIP and web conferencing tools among group meetings is not a basic feature. So, when determining which tool to use and the extent to which it might be used, costs associated with all features must be taken into account. Additionally, consider the integration of the tools with other applications that will be utilized in the online course. For example, some web conferencing tools are integrated within LMSs. The integrated aspect might result in a more effective application of the web conferencing tool than some lesser-used feature, such as file sharing.

Some of the more popular web conferencing tools include Skype (www.skype.com); iChat (http://support.apple.com/kb/HT2515); ooVoo (www.oovoo.com); Google Hangouts (www.google.com/hangouts); Adobe Connect (www.adobe.com/products/adobeconnect/elearning.html); Blackboard Collaborate (www.blackboard.com/Platforms/Collaborate/Products/Blackboard-Collaborate/Web-Conferencing.aspx); GoToMeeting (www.gotomeeting.com/fec); and join.me (http://join.me). Many of these tools are easy to use and provide numerous free features. For example, Skype allows for free file sharing and a certain number of free group videoconferences. Free screen sharing and other communicative tools are offered by join.me, and it has a user-friendly interface. Also, an increasing number of web conferencing tools are now being integrated into other tools, such as the social network Google+, as well as LMSs, providing for increased accessibility and usability.

Web Conferencing Examples. There are numerous ways web conferencing tools can be implemented in large online classes from students' and teachers' perspectives. As a tool to chunk both content and communications, I hold a number of scheduled web conferences throughout many of my courses. In doing this, I make attendance at web conferences either optional or required, depending on the conference's purpose. I use web conferencing tools to conduct virtual office hours, in which students can see and talk to me in real-time to address course issues or content. Web conferencing tools support the inclusion of other more knowledgeable individuals in the teaching and learning environment. Inviting guest speakers, for example, can easily be done using web conferencing tools. Web conferencing tools are also useful in allowing students to illustrate their knowledge of course content in a live, synchronous session, rather than a recorded, asynchronous session.

Conclusion

The current growth of online learning in K–12 schools shows no signs of slowing down. With the increasingly ubiquitous nature of online learning among students from kindergarten through 12th grade, it is essential that educators and educational administrators develop innovative solutions to address growing demands from students and their parents. In this chapter, I discussed pedagogical approaches, including promoting collaborative learning; utilizing both formal and informal assessments; providing opportunities for peer and self-assessments; chunking content and communications; and employing various types of discussion forums. I also identified a number of the traditional and emerging technological tools, including LMSs; wikis; presentation sharing tools; file storage/sharing tools; and VoIP and web conferencing tools; and illustrated how these methods and tools can maximize the benefits of online learning while lightening teachers' workloads and facilitating their management of large online courses. As the online K–12 educational landscape continues to evolve, it will be important for educators to integrate technological applications based on sound pedagogical methods to meet the changing needs of students.

References

Alexander, B. (2006). A new way of innovation for teaching and learning. *Educause Review, 41*(2), 32–44.

Ajjan, II., & Hartshorne, R. (2008). Investigating faculty decisions to adopt web 2.0 technologies: Theory and empirical tests. *The Internet and Higher Education, 11*(2), 71–80.

Allen, I. E., & Seaman, J. (2011). *Going the distance: Online Education in the United States, 2011.* Babson Park, MA: Babson Survey Research Group and Quahog Research Group. Retrieved from www.onlinelearningsurvey.com/reports/goingthedistance.pdf

Black, P., & William, D. (1998). Inside the black box: Raising standards through classroom assessment. *Phi Delta Kappan, 80*(2), 139–148.

Boulos, N. K., and Wheelert, S. (2007). The emerging web 2.0 social software: An enabling suite of sociable technologies in health and health care education. *Health Information and Libraries Journal, 24*(1), 2–23.

Bradford, P., Porciello, M., Balkon, N., & Backus, D. (2007). The Blackboard learning system. *The Journal of Educational Technology Systems, 35,* 301–314.

Brookfield, S. D. (1995). *Becoming a critically reflective teacher.* San Francisco, CA: Jossey-Bass.

Bruner, J. (1996). *Culture of education.* Cambridge, MA: Harvard University Press.

Dearstyne, B. W. (2007). Blogs, mashups, and wikis: Oh my! *Information Management Journal, 41*(4), 24–33.

Ferdig, R. (2007). Examining social software in teacher education. *Journal of Technology and Teacher Education, 15*(1), 5–10.

Hirumi, A. (2003). Get a life: Six tactics for reducing time spent online. *Computers in Schools, 20*(3), 73–101.

Im, Y., & Lee, O. (2003/2004). Pedagogical implications of online discussion for preservice teacher training. *Journal of Research on Technology in Education, 36*(2), 155–170.

Johnson, R. T., & Johnson, D. W. (1986). Action research: Cooperative learning in the science classroom. *Science and Children, 24*(2), 31–32.

Kearsley, G. (2000). *Online education: Learning and teaching in cyberspace.* Belmont, CA: Wadsworth.

Lave, J., & Wenger, E. (1991). *Situated learning: Legitimate peripheral participation.* New York, NY: Cambridge University Press.

Lenhart, A., & Madden, M. (2007). *Social networking websites and teens: An overview.* Pew Internet and American Life Project report. Retrieved from www.pewInternet.org/PPF/r/198/report_display.asp

Madden, M., & Fox, S. (2006). *Riding the waves of "Web 2.0": More than a buzzword, but still not easily defined.* Pew Internet Project, 1–6, (Backgrounder). Retrieved from www.pewinternet.org/~/media//Files/Reports/2006/PIP_Web_2.0.pdf.pdf

Maloney, E. (2007, January). What web 2.0 can teach us about learning. *Chronicle of Higher Education, 25*(18), B26.

Palloff, R. M., & Pratt, K. (2005). *Collaborating online: Learning together in community.* San Francisco, CA: Jossey-Bass.

Pan, C. C., & Sullivan, M. (2005). Promoting synchronous interaction in an eLearning environment. *Technical Horizons in Education Journal, 33*(2), 27–30.

Peterson, E. (2009). Using a wiki to enhance cooperative learning in a real analysis course. *PRIMUS, 19*(1), 18–28.

Siemens, G. (2005). Connectivism: Learning theory for the digital age. *International Journal of Instructional Technology and Distance Learning, 2*(1), Retrieved from www.itdl.org/journal/jan_05/article01.htm

Sturm, M., Kennel, T., McBride, M., & Kelly, M. (2008). The pedagogical implications of web 2.0. In M. Thomas (Ed.), *Handbook of research on web 2.0 and second language learning* (pp. 367–384). Hershey, PA: IGI Publishing.

Vygotsky, L. S. (1978). *Mind in society: The development of higher psychological processes.* Cambridge, MA: Harvard University Press.

Watson, J. F. (2007). *A national primer on K–12 online learning.* Vienna, VA: North American Council for Online Learning.

CHAPTER 2

Podcasting in Education
Practices and Precautions

John H. Curry

THIS CHAPTER PROVIDES a resource to educators and instructional designers who want to learn more about podcasting. The chapter provides a basic definition of podcasting and also provides links to a number of different podcasting examples from K–12 classrooms. Differing levels of podcast integration are defined. For those who want to create their own podcasts, practices and precautions for podcasting are discussed. In addition, this chapter provides information and links aimed to help teachers and students create podcasts. Resources are broken down into the following categories: creating podcasts, hosting podcasts, free music resources for podcasts, and other general resources.

With the advent of so many new technologies, teachers must increasingly compete for the attention of students. Whether they are texting, playing the newest video game, or listening to their MP3 players, students can't seem to get away from their electronics. While these electronic devices can seem like distractions, they can also become tools for teachers. One such technology that can be harnessed and used for educational benefit is a podcast.

Podcasts might sound scary or seem hard to do, but they are easy to create, edit, and publish. The term podcast simply implies a file, or a broadcast, that is "playable on demand," hence the shortened form podcast. Along the same lines, a vodcast is formed from the first letters of the words "video on demand" plus "cast," meaning a video podcast, shortened to vodcast. No longer do those with fancy equipment control the airwaves. Creating your own podcast can truly be as simple as dialing a phone number, speaking into your phone, and hanging up. Podcasts can obviously be much more complex than that, but this chapter will give you some pointers and things to look out for when you create your podcasts. It will also provide you with plenty of samples to listen to and resources to get you started.

Why use podcasts at all? Podcasts provide a rich resource to instructors on virtually any subject, and instructors who are looking for another access point to their instruction will be surprised at how many ideas there are for podcast integration. An English teacher might use them to have students listen to a poet reading his or her own work. A foreign language teacher might use them to work on pronunciation or listening comprehension. A science or math teacher might use them as a review for a particularly challenging concept. A social studies teacher might have students listen to travel podcasts about different countries or have students listen to historical recordings. The possibilities truly seem endless.

Levels of Integration

There is no one specific approach to integrating technology into the classroom that fits all instructional situations. Individual instructors have to make their own decisions about what kinds of podcasts they are going to use or create and why and when they are going to use them. Simply creating a podcast for your class without having a specific reason for doing so might be novel, but it will have no real educational sustainability, and you and your students will probably soon leave it by the wayside. Your podcasts should add to or otherwise enhance what you are already doing in your class, not take away from it.

While there are a number of different scales of technology integration that have been published, there are really just two levels of integration when it comes to technology in the classroom. The first is teacher-centered integration. In the case of podcasts, teachers at the teacher-centered level find and listen to podcasts for their own professional development. The second level is student-centered integration and can be broken into two sublevels. The first would be the students listening to podcasts to better access content. The second, much more powerful, level is students creating their own podcasts not only to help others access the content, but also to participate in the educational conversation (Curry & Buckner, 2012). Having the students create their own podcasts gets them to interact with the content on a deeper level and makes them accountable for the quality of their work to their peers and to their instructor.

Podcasting Examples

There are so many podcasts available that it is impossible to review them all. The following are examples of podcasts created by teachers and students. Take the opportunity to listen to examples of both, and reflect on the depth of the educational experience for the students in each case.

Instructor-created podcasts

Karen's Mashups: Compilations of Digital Content for K–12 Educators:
www.K–12handhelds.com/mashups
> This website features numerous mashups, or compilations, of different digital content that would be of interest to many educators and their classes. It is easily accessible, and the content is well produced.

Children's Fun Storytime:
https://itunes.apple.com/us/podcast/childrens-fun-storytime-podcast/id207671602
> One of many podcasts in which stories are read aloud for children, this one's focus is mainly on the classics, from summarized versions of Alice in Wonderland to many of Grimm's Fairy Tales.

Poem of the Day: https://itunes.apple.com/us/podcast/poem-of-the-day/id270054094
> When it comes to poetry, few experiences are as enjoyable as hearing the author read his or her own work. A simple search of the iTunes poetry site reveals numerous podcasts for a poem a day. Some have the author reading the work, and others discuss a certain poem every day or week. Be careful before you start checking these out; time goes by quickly!

The Science Show for Kids: www.learnoutloud.com/Podcast-Directory/Science/-/
Why-The-Science-Show-For-Kids-Podcast/23127%23plink
> In this podcast, Dave Brodbeck answers science questions from children. You can also access his blog and other science resources from this website.

Tech Time with Mr. S: http://weskids.com/techtime0708/?cat=3
> In this podcast, Bob Sprankle, technology integrator at Wells Elementary School in Wells, Maine, discusses different technologies and their uses. He's fun to listen to, and the site offers access to archives of past shows.

Student-created podcasts

Radio WillowWeb: http://mps.wes.schoolfusion.us (click the tab for Radio WillowWeb)
> In 2005, students of all grades at Willowdale Elementary School in Omaha, Nebraska, started broadcasting information on a wide variety of topics. Radio WillowWeb is perhaps the most famous of all K–12 student-created podcasts. After tuning in to listen to several Willowcasts, you and your students may be encouraged to create your own podcasts!

Coulee Kids:

https://itunes.apple.com/us/podcast/a-school-in-the-coulee-podcast/id79169064
With regular visitors from all over the world, the seventh graders at Longfellow Middle School in La Crosse, Wisconsin, participate in this podcast as part of their writing class, but they often include material from other content areas.

ColeyCast: http://coleycast.blogspot.com
Billed as the "official" podcast of the fifth grade students in room 34 at Tovashal Elementary School in Murietta, California, this podcast allows the students to share highlights of the things they are learning in their classroom.

KidCast: Podcasting in the Classroom: www.intelligenic.com/blog/?page_id=2
Another podcast with almost five years worth of episodes, the KidCast podcast has an enormous amount of information on how to do your own podcast, but even more exciting, this is the home to the KidCast Podcasting Awards (www.intelligenic.com/blog/?cat=25). Visit this site to hear award-winning student-created podcasts!

Our City Podcast: http://learninginhand.com/ourcity
The Our City podcast is a place where students from all over posted their own podcasts about the town they lived in. Although this is an archive and no longer adding new material, this is a good example of a podcast by kids for kids.

Podcasting Practices and Precautions

While creating podcasts is relatively easy, there are some things you can do that will greatly enhance the quality of your product. The nice thing about podcasts is that you really don't need a lot of fancy equipment to create them. If you have a high-end computer and all the toys that go with it, of course you can use it, yet you can call from your home phone—not even a cell phone—and still create a good podcast with fine sound quality. Each of these suggestions and precautions apply equally no matter what you're using to record your podcasts. Follow them, and you'll sound like a professional.

Tip 1. Plan it out—write a script

One of the biggest mistakes that novice podcasters make is simply to sit down and start speaking into the microphone. While podcasting truly is easy, unprepared, extemporaneous recordings are not advisable. Unless you are an extremely gifted off-the-cuff speaker, recording without a plan can lead to podcasts that are merely recorded ramblings. The best way to avoid a podcast full of awkward silences or a lot of "umms … " and repeated fillers, such as "you know" and "like," is to have some sort of script written out. If nothing else, thorough notes to follow will give you a sense of direction as you record and keep you on track.

Some people like to write out the full script—word for word—before they record. Others will simply write and follow an outline. Do whatever you are comfortable with, but if you follow a script, you'll sound more professional and spend less total time on your podcasts.

Tip 2. Keep it simple

Podcasts don't have to be hard. Yes, you can make them complex by adding all sorts of enhanced features, like chapters, hyperlinks, or graphics (yes, graphics!), but if you're not comfortable with the fancy enhancements, then don't add them. The content is what is going to determine the success of your podcast, not the bells and whistles you can add to it technologically. At the same time, keep the length short. The likelihood that listeners are going to bear with you for an hour to hear what you could have said in 15 minutes is small. Be succinct, and get to the point. Keep each one short and simple.

Tip 3. Have fun!

Podcasting isn't meant to be a burden; it's easy, and it's empowering. So have fun while you do it. Dress up or dress down; it doesn't really matter. But if you're uncomfortable or aren't enjoying the process, these feelings will come through to your listeners by your manner of speaking.

Tip 4. Enlist co-hosts and guest speakers

Are you tired of doing all the talking? Then don't! It's great to break things up and have co-hosts or guest speakers on your podcast. It's okay to give up control once in a while. You are not the expert on every topic—so why not bring one in? It is surprising how effective a guest speaker can be. Ask the expert to deliver a presentation on a topic related to what your class is studying, or interview the expert. Enlisting local people to share their expertise can add another dimension to a podcast, moving it from the teacher lecturing to the students listening to a conversation or presentation about a topic. But be prepared. When you have someone else on the podcast, your preparation for the discussion is extremely important. Make sure you have prepared meaningful questions (no "yes" or "no" questions) that will further the discussion. If you think it's bad listening to one person ramble or saying, "ummm …," imagine how boring it would be for your students to listen to two unprepared people.

Tip 5. Skip citations

Unless you're really catering to an academic crowd, there's no reason to try to impress anyone with scholarly citations. Most people enjoy listening to an informal discussion rather than a scholarly lecture, and that's especially true in a podcast. However, if you have relied heavily on one or several sources for a podcast or quoted extensively from an author's work, you can mention that these sources are listed on the podcast's URL for those who would like to explore the subject further.

Tip 6. Keep it quiet

When you record your podcast, be aware of your surroundings. No one wants to hear your phone ring or a door slam in the middle of the podcast. Find a quiet place where you can record unin-terrupted. Turn everything you don't need off. Don't sit in that squeaky chair you got from your mom. When you record, be careful of the microphone. Don't sit too close to the mike, or all the

/p/ and /b/ sounds will be like explosions in the listeners' ears, and the /sh/, /s/, and /th/ sounds will come across like static. Extraneous sounds can be distracting in a podcast. If your recording contains too many, listeners will begin to focus on the ambient sounds and your exaggerated speech sounds rather than your content.

Tip 7. Make your music interesting

As crazy as it seems, buffer music, or the music that begins and ends the podcast, can be very important to the success of your podcast. Keep it age-appropriate and appropriate for the topic. In the past, when creating podcasts for my students, I've allowed them to submit music requests for our buffers. Then they all tuned in to see if their songs were selected. It was exciting for them to hear a shout-out to them and their requests. However, be careful if you use music requests because this can severely impact your ability to reuse the podcasts due to copyright.

Tip 8. Plan for reusability

Podcasts are fun and easy to make, but that doesn't necessarily mean that they are done quickly. So when creating your podcast, plan ahead for reusability. Record it so it can be used again next term or next year. It's pretty frustrating to re-listen to a podcast and catch yourself making some reference to a current event relevant to the time when you were recording the podcast that now has no relevance.

Tip 9. Don't be afraid to edit

When they first start to podcast, most people are just happy to have recorded and posted something. And while that is a big accomplishment, once you become more relaxed and accustomed to the process, don't be afraid to edit out mistakes. When I first started podcasting, I would get frustrated when I made a mistake and start all over again. Not now. If I make a mistake, I just keep on talking, and I make a note of the time of the error so it's easy for me to find afterward. Then when I'm done, I go back over the recording to edit out the errors. Editing is as easy as highlighting and selecting the part with the error and hitting the delete button. This simple process makes my podcasts sound much more professional. If you get stuck with a problem while editing, you can always use the help function, but I prefer searching YouTube for tutorial videos on editing podcasts.

Tip 10. Copyright

How can someone get into copyright trouble in a podcast? The most serious transgressions occur when people use copyrighted buffer music and play the entire song. Remember, you are not allowed to play a whole song, but you may play a few seconds of it to introduce an educational podcast. With plenty of places online to download copyright-free music (see the list later in this chapter), teachers should never have this problem.

Tip 11. Feedback

We all like to feel like we do excellent work the first time we do it, but feedback is really important if we want to do a good job. Ask your listeners if you are rambling, if you are enunciating your words, or if you are even making sense in general. It's not a bad thing to be told what you can improve on, and when your listeners feel like they are being listened to themselves, then they have more buy-in to the entire process and podcast.

Podcasting Resources

There are a seemingly unlimited number of resources available to help someone who wants to get involved with podcasting. To simply listen to podcasts, one only needs to access a podcast directory like Apple's iTunes and search for the desired topic. However, iTunes isn't the only directory. There are several on the web worth checking out, such as Podcastdirectory.com, Podcast Alley (www.podcastalley.com), Podseek (www.podseek.net), or podfeed (www.podfeed.net). Each of these has a searchable directory and a number of podcasts on many different topics. But to get into creating your own professional-sounding podcasts, you'll need an idea of where to begin. This section will review some resources available to help you.

Creating Podcasts

GarageBand: www.apple.com/ilife/garageband
> GarageBand is by far the easiest program to use to create a podcast. However, it is only for Macintosh computers and comes as a standard application with each machine. There is also an iOS version.

Audacity: http://audacity.sourceforge.net
> Audacity is a free, open source program that functions much like GarageBand. It's user-friendly and accessible for a novice as well as an expert. It can be a little tricky to save your first podcast, but once you've done it, it's a breeze. One of the benefits of using an open source program is that there is plenty of support available in online forums. Available for both Mac and PC.

Adobe Audition: www.adobe.com/products/audition/main.html
> Audition is Adobe's answer to GarageBand. It has a lot of advanced features and will certainly provide a lot of options to a more advanced user. It's expensive, and unless you really want some advanced features, I'd go with something else.

Podcasting Tools: www.podcasting-tools.com
> This repository site has links to options for just about everything you could ever want or need to learn about podcasting including how to create your own.

FeedForAll: RSS Feed Creation Tool: www.feedforall.com/tools-for-podcasting.htm
> This repository site has a lot of articles about podcasting as well as links to different resources, including podcasting tools.

Hosting Podcasts

Once you have created your own podcasts, you'll need somewhere to store them so others can access them. Each of the following sites either hosts (provides server space for storage) podcasts or is a directory where you can have your podcast listed so others can access it. Some also have links to resources.

iTunes: www.apple.com/itunes—Directory

Podcast Alley: www.podcastalley.com—Directory and resources

Educate: Podcasts for educators, schools and colleges: http://recap.ltd.uk/podcasting—Directory

Podbus.com: www.podbus.com—Host

podcastdirectory.com: The portal for audio and video podcasts: www.podcastdirectory.com—Directory

Free Music Resources for Podcasts

The biggest copyright offender in podcasting is the music that people use as buffers or as backgrounds. This should never happen! First, as teachers, we need to model ethical behavior, obey the law, and make sure that we comply with copyright law. Second, there is so much free, legal music to use, there is no excuse not to use podsafe music. For a good explanation of what podsafe music is and how to use it, see the Podsafe Music page of the FeedForAll website (www.feedforall.com/how-to-locate-podsafe-music.htm). The following websites advertise copyright-free music or audio for educational use.

Music Alley: www.musicalley.com

Podsafe Audio: www.podsafeaudio.com

freeacidloops: www.freeacidloops.net

ACIDplanet: www.acidplanet.com/downloads/8packs

Looperman: www.looperman.com/loops

Freeplay Music: http://freeplaymusic.com

Platinum Loops: www.platinumloops.com/free_loops.shtml

The Daily .WAV: www.dailywav.com

Future Wave Shaper: www.futurewaveshaper.com

FindSounds: www.findsounds.com

Sonnyboo: http://sonnyboo.com/music/music.htm

Loopgalaxy: www.loopgalaxy.com

Other Resources

Now that you know where to find information to help you create podcasts, what you'll need, and where to get it, below are some websites that contain some beneficial general information about podcasting.

Apple Education: www.apple.com/education/podcasting

Apple's Education website contains information on how to create and disseminate podcasts, as well as case studies so you can see what others are doing.

Learning in Hand: http://learninginhand.com/podcasting

This user-friendly site is written without a lot of jargon and is a rich resource about all things that have to do with mobile learning. It contains information on how to create podcasts and on how to find, subscribe, and just listen to them. This site also breaks mobile learning into different technologies, such as iPods, iPads, Netbooks, or PDAs. I highly suggest visiting this one.

Education Podcast Network: www.aboutus.org/Epnweb.org

The EPN is a vast directory of educational podcasts on a variety of subjects. You can browse the directory by grade level or by subject.

iPodder: www.ipodder.org

This site has an extensive directory on a number of subjects as well as information about how to create, publish, and promote your own podcasts.

Podcasting Plus: http://engage.wisc.edu/podcasting

The University of Wisconsin-Madison's repository on everything podcasting includes how-to guides, award winners, teaching and learning examples, and copyright information.

Teach with Tech: K–12 Podcasting:

http://teachwtech.blogspot.com/2006/02/episode-7-preview-k-12-podcasting-and.html

Teach with Tech is a wonderful podcast about technology integration in general, produced by the Indiana University School of Education Instructional Consulting Office. This episode deals with K–12 podcasting.

A Final Word

Above all, remember this: podcasting is fun! It's time-consuming, yes, but it can be rewarding as well. Make sure that when you create your podcasts, you have a specific reason for doing so. Don't just use "technology for technology's sake." When you have a sound purpose behind technology integration, your podcasts can help your instruction be more effective, efficient, and engaging. Also remember that it doesn't take much effort for your podcasts to sound professional. Experiment. Practice. In no time, you'll not only feel more comfortable with your own production process, but you'll also be producing instructional materials that are engaging to your listeners in and outside your classroom.

References

Curry, J. H., & Buckner, D. L. (2012). A practical guide for integrating technology into social studies instruction. In D. Polly, C. Mims, & K. Persichitte (Eds.), *Developing technology-rich teacher education programs: Key issues* (pp. 378–392). Hershey, PA: IGI Global.

CHAPTER 3

Virtual Worlds
and Their Educational Potential

John Neely and Zane L. Berge

INCREASING NUMBERS OF PEOPLE are spending time in virtual online worlds to socialize, work together on projects, conduct business, and learn. By 2011, nearly 1.2 billion people had registered to participate in one of these immersive three-dimensional (3-D) environments, a 36% increase from 2010. With their ability to engage learners, encourage collaboration, and promote self-directed exploration, virtual worlds have such great potential for learning that professional educators need to understand how they can be used as classroom tools. Without making a large financial investment, educators should begin to experiment with how to leverage them as an effective learning technology. They will find that virtual worlds provide a powerful environment for role-play and simulation, a platform where skills can be developed safely and inexpensively before they are implemented in the real world. While virtual worlds can provide rich and authentic instructor-led classroom experiences, the most successful uses of virtual worlds can be as environments for student-led, informal learning—places to explore, socialize, create, and experience life through alternate lenses.

Millions of people each day escape their real worlds and travel into alternate, often strange, online virtual worlds to have fun, meet people, conduct business, and even learn. The numbers making the journey down metaphorical rabbit holes are growing each day. By 2011, an estimated 1.185 billion people had registered in one of the 175 virtual worlds that are either live or in beta testing, up from 867 million registered users at the beginning of 2010 (Kzero, 2011). Second Life, the most popular virtual world, reported that 750,000 people spent 150 million hours in its 3-D space during the fourth quarter of 2010 (Linden Lab, 2011). In its tenth anniversary press release, Second Life reports that 36 million accounts have been created over the past 10 years and that users have spent the equivalent of 217,266 years in Second Life (Linden Lab, 2013a). Habbo Hotel, a virtual world targeted to 10- to 15-year-olds, reports more than 200 million registered users (Habbo Hotel, 2011). Moshi Monsters, designed for 5- to 10-year olds, had 20 million members in 2010 compared with 12 million the year before (Keegen, 2010).

This increase in participation has accompanied a surge in interest among learning professionals about the potential of virtual worlds as a learning technology. More than 140 higher education institutions (Linden Lab, 2013a) and nearly 120 corporations (New Business Horizons, 2011) have a presence in Second Life, using this virtual 3-D world as a place to hold class, collaborate, explore, role-play, and test new ideas in a safe but compelling way. Academic institutions that have ventured into the virtual world include Harvard University, Ball State University, Western Kentucky University, and the University of Texas. Early corporate adopters include IBM, Dell, Cisco, Mazda, and Intel. Virtual worlds have also begun to attract the attention of K–12 educators. Suffern Middle School in New York and Exeter Township School District in Pennsylvania are two pioneers in the use of this emerging technology.

All of these early adopters are drawn by the virtual worlds' facility to create an environment to enhance experiential learning, allowing individuals to practice skills, try new ideas, and learn from their mistakes. Educators also see the appeal of virtual worlds to the so-called "digital native" generation. This generation, who are increasingly part of the workforce, expects technology to take a central role in any learning environment. Technology—including video games, cell phones, MP3 players, text messaging, and now virtual worlds—has been a central and integrated part of their lives since they were born.

Virtual worlds may not be a transformative technology on the level of television or the Internet, but they clearly have potential as a learning tool. They are an emerging technology at the same place in their development lifecycle as the Internet was in the early 1990s. Learning professionals are both excited and perplexed about how to best use these 3-D environments to enhance learning, just as they were 20 years ago when the Internet was a relatively new technology. This chapter explores virtual worlds, including their potential as a learning technology and the challenges that remain before they will be widely adopted by K–12 educators and higher education schools, as well as by corporate training departments.

Virtual Worlds

Virtual worlds, also known as multi-user virtual environments (MUVEs), provide an immersive, 3-D environment that operates over the Internet, giving access to anyone in the world who has the required computer equipment and a high-speed connection. Avatars that represent users can move around the 3-D space and communicate in real time with other avatars. The avatar serves as the user's alter ego, with online participants creating and selecting the avatar's name, gender, hairstyle, body type, and clothing.

Avatars navigate through the virtual world either by walking in a traditional real-world manner or by teleporting from one place to another at the speed of light. The constraints of distance are removed in the virtual world. Avatars hop to and from places just like people surf from site to site on the World Wide Web.

Avatars interact in real time with one another through the actions of their real-life puppet-masters. Conversations are usually conducted by text chat, although voice technology is increasingly used. Second Life, for example, employs Voice over Internet Protocol (VoIP) technology to give users, through their avatars, the powerful ability to speak in real time with other users. Adding to the authenticity of the experience, voices from avatars on the right come to users through the right speaker, and the voices of avatars at a distance are softer than those nearby.

Avatars function differently in non-gaming virtual worlds from the ways they do in the virtual worlds provided by massive multiplayer online games (MMOGs). In an MMOG, such as the popular World of Warcraft, the avatar has a fixed mission to complete. In non-gaming virtual worlds, avatars have not been programmed to accomplish central or overarching themes or particular goals or missions. It is up to the avatar, guided by its real-life puppeteer, to create the world that the human role-player wants. Second Life, launched in 2003, and *3DMee*, which started in 2007, are two examples of non-gaming virtual worlds.

Powerful tools are available to construct that world. Users in Second Life and *3DMee* are provided with simple geometric shapes and given the flexibility to change the characteristics of those shapes and combine them to generate a limitless set of possible 3-D objects—including cars, buildings, guitars, furniture, telescopes, molecules, and cats—anything that the imagination conjures up and the builder has the talent to build. To make objects dynamic and interactive, the builder needs to write scripts. These sections of code attach to objects and modify their behavior. These tools provide for a creative and industrious society of builders. In spite of the learning curve, more than 50% of Second Life residents attempt to create objects each month (Ondrejka, 2007).

The 3-D environment comprises valuable objects and entities that can be built by the collaborative efforts of one or more fellow residents. "Members of the wiki movement may envision Wikipedia becoming Wikitechture, with avatars co-creating things in 3-D space and learning all along the way" (Cross, O'Driscoll, & Trondsen, 2007, para. 11). What is unique is that the collaboration occurs via real-time processing of data and in a shared 3-D space. With wikis and blogs—examples of collaborative, user-developed information sources in the 2-D world of the Internet—the creation is sequential and asynchronous. One person makes an entry, and at a later time another person adds a comment or makes another entry (Ondrejka, 2007). In contrast, within the non-gaming MUVEs, creative and collaborative efforts occur as they would in the real world—in real time.

Objects developed in the virtual world can be used by the creator, given away, or sold. It is the latter—the business side of MUVEs—that has helped fuel much of their growth. Using Linden Dollars in Second Life, which are purchased with real currency at a floating exchange rate, users buy and sell land, objects, and services. In 2009, sales of land, objects, and artifacts totaled about $500 million in Second Life (Keegen, 2010).

Educational Potential

Virtual worlds provide an immersive, authentic environment for both formal, instructor-directed learning and informal, student-directed learning.

Formal Learning

A traditional classroom can be emulated in the virtual world with students meeting at a scheduled time to hear a lecture accompanied by PowerPoint slides, hold discussions, and complete activities as they would in a brick and mortar classroom. Virtual worlds, using this delivery model, essentially provide a 3-D and more satisfying version of the 2-D, synchronous, distance-learning classroom supplied by Webex, Adobe Connect, and others. "Second Life gives us the capability to really have a classroom experience with the students," says Rebecca Nesson, who co-teaches a course at Harvard Law School called CyberOne: Law in the Court of Public Opinion. "It really changes the way the classroom conversation proceeds because you have a sense of all of these people being there, participating in one way or another. … It somehow gives people a sense of community that they're not by themselves doing this" (cited in Lamb, 2006, para. 7). IBM is one example of a private corporation that sees the benefit of using Second Life for formal learning. They are starting to use it as a 3-D replacement of their existing 2-D virtual classrooms (Hall & Nguyen, 2007).

Informal Learning

Learning organizations that would like to move into the virtual world will, at first no doubt, be tempted to use this alternate environment to host their classrooms because they are familiar with and know how to manage the virtual-world model. However, the real power of virtual worlds as a learning technology is not in their ability to improve upon the current virtual classroom. Instead, virtual worlds' power lies in their ability to provide an environment for informal learning—a learner-directed model of exploration and knowledge development. The opportunities provided by virtual worlds for learner-directed problem solving, collaboration, exploration, and discovery fit well with constructivist learning theory, which stresses a problem-solving approach to learning, experiential learning, and ownership of the learning process by learners. Virtual worlds provide learners with the tools to collaborate and *construct* knowledge as they immerse themselves in what these alternate worlds have to offer. Bob Mosher, a director at Microsoft Learning, contends that although "more formal forms of instruction such as the classroom and e-learning will be around for years, it's becoming more and more important to watch and harness the more informal methodologies that our students are utilizing" (Mosher, 2004, para. 2). Virtual worlds have become one more important way for organizations to harness informal learning and enable learners to construct their own knowledge. Several powerful learning applications are available in virtual worlds that can be part of learning that is either formal and instructor-directed or informal and student-directed.

Storytelling

Virtual worlds allow K–12 students to more fully develop their creative and storytelling skills, either as a stand-alone experience for individual students or as part of a teacher-mediated experience. Avatar Storytellers is a virtual world developed by WiloStar3D and designed specifically for classroom students ages 9 to 12. Students create and customize their own avatars and then write virtual-world quests using unique avatar characters. The 3-D environment simulates the creative storytelling process by encouraging students to create interesting characters and engaging plotlines (WiloStar3D, 2011).

Role-Playing

Virtual worlds allow learners to adopt different personae and reflect on how others react to the alternative personae. For some it is transformative. In a Massachusetts-based project called live2give, nine adults with cerebral palsy spent time in Second Life and experienced life as others without their disability do in the real world. "Many of the real-world challenges are bypassed in Second Life," said June-Marie Mahay, who works with the nine at an adult day-care center. "Fewer folks have a problem hanging out with them, which is quite the opposite in real life. They felt stigmatized by their disabilities, (which) kept them from the normal social integration we take for granted. Second Life removes both of these things" (cited in Terdiman, 2005, para. 6).

Role-playing in Second Life enabled one anonymous blogger to explore ageism. Turning her avatar into a senior citizen, she was surprised at the negative reactions she experienced in the virtual world. "I am disheartened by the ageism I experienced in SL … especially after finding SL to be such a friendly environment before my transformation" (EdGames, 2007, para. 5).

Such role-playing would be a powerful addition to any high school or college class on diversity in society. What might one learn by being another race in Second Life? By following another religion? By being a different gender? By living as a disabled person?

Role-playing within a 3-D environment can also be a powerful way to augment lesson plans in K–12 classrooms. Middle school students at Suffern Middle School in Suffern, New York, have taken a virtual field trip to a recreation of Ellis Island and the Statue of Liberty, enabling them to role-play the immigrant experience (Sheehy, 2009a). An island has been created in Second Life that recreates the world imagined by Shakespeare for Macbeth. High school literature students are able to role-play key scenes and interact dynamically with the 3-D environment, from a ride on the back of a raven, to a psychotic sword fight with Macbeth's demons (Virtual Macbeth, 2011).

Simulation

Virtual worlds allow learners to obtain skills, competencies, knowledge, and behaviors by interacting with realistic objects and with others in situations that are similar to real life. Skills can be developed in a safe environment before they are implemented in the real world. One distinct advantage of virtual worlds is that objects that others can live in, sit on, pick up, and so on can be created at a very low cost. David E. Stone, an MIT research fellow, created simulations in Second Life in three days for $350. These same simulations would have taken six months and $60,000 to complete using another platform (Mollman, 2007).

Examples abound of how virtual worlds can be used for skill development. A physics professor at Elon University has created an authentic telescope trainer to teach his students the proper order for adjusting the focus knobs on a real telescope (Kemp & Livingstone, 2006). Architecture students at Montana State University use Second Life to learn how to design and create structures, interiors, and furniture (Magid, 2007). Students at Suffern Middle School created a 3-D model of the solar system as part of a unit on planetary science (Sheehy, 2009b).

Other simulations place learners in a different time and place. A computer scientist at Vassar College has developed a faithful 3-D digital recreation of the Sistine Chapel (Vassar College, 2007). An Egyptian archeologist has created a museum of Egyptian artifacts and architecture (Linden, 2006).

Builders in virtual worlds can change scales and perspectives when building objects used in simulations. For example, one's avatar can walk in and out of an atom or fly through the aorta of a human heart. This modeling capability is a real advantage for skills-based training, according to Paul Steinberg, project manager at Intel Software Solutions Group, who extols the benefits of students being able to interact with a large-scale, 3-D computer chip (cited in Grondstedt, 2007).

Interacting with objects is not the only use of simulations in a virtual world. Complex scenarios involving collaboration among participants can be developed for learning purposes. Delta L, a training company, has developed a team-building simulation within Second Life. Participants work together to complete a simple task, and then they are asked to step back and reflect on their teamwork abilities and attitudes (Newswire Today, 2007). The Center for the Advancement of Distance Education at the University of Illinois at Chicago has developed a first-responder training program for natural or man-made disasters. Participants in the simulation are asked to implement a real-life emergency plan in the virtual world (Girard, 2007). At the University of Kansas Medical Center, a medical clinic has been constructed on Second Life and is used by learners to practice applying patient encounter strategies (Antonacci & Modaress, 2008).

One can envision numerous uses of virtual world simulations in a corporate training setting, including simulating on the job harassment as part of a sexual harassment course; practicing sales skills; simulating a disaster as part of a course teaching employees their roles in an emergency; and practicing interviewing skills.

The virtual world in and of itself can be viewed as a microcosm or simulation of real life and, therefore, is fertile ground for learning. For example, observing how business is conducted, land is bought and sold, and products are marketed could be a powerful addition to a business course. Observing how groups form and interact with each other in a MUVE might illustrate some powerful lessons in a high school sociology course, particularly after students have participated in a virtual environment.

Collaboration and Communication

One cannot ignore the power of virtual worlds to provide environments for meaningful communication. Conversations take place in real time and in an authentic 3-D space, where one can use one's actual voice (as opposed to text messaging). Many—perhaps most—MUVE participants go to the virtual world to interact socially with others and to network, not explicitly to learn or conduct business. Virtual worlds for certain people may actually enhance communication. Eryn Grant, who completed a study of the social order in virtual worlds while pursuing a doctorate at Queensland University of Technology's School of Humanities, describes how participation facilitates connecting with strangers:

> There are not many places we go in the world where we are guaranteed social contact, in real life it is harder and less likely that you will go up to a stranger and start a conversation (cited in Science Daily, 2008).

In Harvard Law School's course CyberOne: Law in the Court of Public Opinion, students were given the choice of attending class in the real or virtual world. Because of the "pseudonymity" provided by their students' avatars in Second Life, the professors found that students felt less threatened and preferred asking questions in the virtual environment (Ondrejka, 2007). William James, an extension school student working toward a citation in legal studies said, "Some people don't have the confidence to interact in a classroom, especially with one of the world's greatest law professors, but can do so in Second Life" (Nolan, 2006, para. 10). The pseudonymity provided by the avatar may be liberating for many reticent students, giving them confidence to communicate with their peers and the course's co-instructors.

Organizations have begun to leverage virtual worlds as a communication tool. IBM, for example, is using Second Life to replace webinars and videoconferencing (Gronstedt, 2007). One would expect that others would follow IBM's lead and start to use the virtual world to encourage small-group collaboration and as an enhanced method for conducting meetings. Corporations could use the virtual world as a collaboration and communication forum for other business purposes. Coaching and mentoring, employee orientation, job interviewing, and employee recruiting are all activities that can and do take place in this 3-D environment.

Challenges

As with most emerging technologies, virtual worlds are experiencing growing pains. A number of issues need to be addressed before full-scale adoption is possible.

The potential for exposure to pornography and other inappropriate content has prevented K–12 schools and some higher education institutions and corporate training departments from participating in the "full-and-open" virtual worlds. Second Life established a gated community called the Teen Grid, which provided a safe environment for middle and high school students. However, the company discontinued the grid in the summer of 2010, leaving K–12 schools scrambling for an alternative (Sheehy, 2011). Some schools have chosen to move to a virtual world built using OpenSimulator, an open source software that enables the development of multi-user virtual worlds with the same features and characteristics of Second Life. Schools can either build and host their own virtual worlds or lease virtual worlds built and hosted by a growing number of vendors, such as ReactionGrid. Peggy Sheehy, a media specialist at Suffern Middle School, Suffern, New York, reports her more recent experience: "OpenSim allows a virtual world platform that schools can run for free on their own servers or can get hosted inexpensively and quickly—by a growing number of providers. The space can be up and running within a day, which is a large part of the reason for OpenSim's appeal" (2011, para. 5).

Participation in virtual worlds is also inhibited by its steep learning curve relative to other distance learning technologies. New users need to learn how to create an avatar, make it walk and teleport, chat with other avatars, and use the other basic "survival" tools available in the virtual world. Some aspects of virtual worlds have a steeper learning curve than others. Learning how to build objects takes time and can be a real challenge for many new users.

Providing access to the visually impaired should be an important consideration for all educators. This is particularly important if the learning project is sponsored by federal government funding, which requires that new electronic and information technologies meet certain access standards as defined in Section 508 of the 1973 Rehabilitation Act as amended in 1998. Second Life would not adhere to Section 508 requirements. Navigation in its 3-D world would be impossible for the blind or near blind. In addition, the text chat does not work with a screen reader (Kemp & Livingstone, 2006).

Vendors are just now starting to address the technical challenges involved in integrating virtual worlds with the learning management systems that are used in K–12 education, higher education, and corporate learning to track student behavior and progress (Berking & Gallagher, 2013). It is likely that these challenges will be fully overcome in the not so distant future. The situation-linked object-oriented dynamic learning environment called Sloodle (www.sloodle.org) is open source software that can be used to develop links from the Moodle learning management system (https://moodle.org) to Second Life and to virtual worlds developed by OpenSimulator. Moodle, a free web application, is a learning management system used at many higher education institutions to create online learning sites.

Additionally, security is an issue for some corporations that are considering using a "full and open" virtual world operating outside the organization's firewall. Corporations will be hesitant to conduct training that might expose its trade secrets and sensitive information. The alternative is to use a "closed" virtual world that lies within the company's firewall, which is developed using OpenSimulator or leased from a growing list of vendors.

Conclusion

Mitch Kapor, founder of Lotus Corporation, may have been guilty of hyperbole when he stated that virtual worlds are "a disruptive technology on the level of the personal computer or the Internet" (quoted in Wallace, 2006, para. 2). In any event, virtual worlds clearly provide organizations with a potentially powerful learning technology to add to their toolkits. With their ability to engage learners, encourage collaboration, and promote self-directed exploration, virtual worlds have too much potential for professional educators to ignore.

Virtual worlds are an emerging technology, at the same point in their maturation cycle as the Internet was in the early 1990s. K–12 schools, higher education institutions, and corporate training departments should, like Alice in Wonderland, follow the rabbit down into the hole and investigate and experiment with these other worlds.

The question for learning professionals is how to better leverage this new learning tool. One approach is to transport the instructor-led classroom to a virtual world, where many students are likely to have a richer learning experience than 2-D synchronous platforms are able to provide. However, organizations should realize that "a virtual classroom with virtual students and a virtual PowerPoint deck is not the end-game for learning in virtual worlds" (Cross, O'Driscoll, & Trondsen, 2007, para. 6). Virtual worlds are more than just a better way to provide synchronous distance learning. The most powerful use of virtual worlds will be as a "sandbox" for students' self-directed, informal learning—an environment that encourages and stimulates exploration, experimentation, practice, and testing of new ideas. As Sheehy says, virtual worlds reintroduce students to "… curiosity, playfulness, risk-taking, and experimentation that embraces 'failure' as a *necessary* step toward success…" (Sheehy, 2011, para. 35).

References

Aldrich, C. (2011). Clark Aldrich's style guide for serious games and simulations. Retrieved from www.networkedblogs.com/blog/clark_aldrichs_style_guide_for_serious_games_and_simulations

Antonacci, D. M., & Modress, N. (2008). Envisioning the educational possibilities of user-created virtual worlds. *AACE Journal, 16*(2), 115–126. Retrieved from www.editlib.org/p/24253

Berking, P., & Gallagher, S. (2013, May 14). Choosing a learning management system [White paper]. Advanced Distributed Learning (ADL) Co-Laboratories. Retrieved from www.adlnet.gov/wp-content/uploads/2013/05/Choosing_an_LMS.pdf

Cross, J., O'Driscoll, T., & Trondsen, E. (2007, March). Another life: Virtual worlds as tools for learning. *eLearn Magazine.* Retrieved from http://elearnmag.acm.org/featured.cfm?aid=1235515

EdGames (2007, November 10). Agism [sic] in Second Life. Blog created by the learning community of EDTEC 670 at San Diego State University. Retrieved from http://edweb.sdsu.edu/courses/edtec670/edgames/2007_11_01_archive.htm; (23rd post).

Girard, N. (2007, October 25). The e-learning adventure. *TechNewsWorld.* Retrieved from www.technewsworld.com/story/59988.html

Gronstedt, A. (2007). Second Life produces real training results. *Training and Development, 61*(8), 44–49. Retrieved from www.gronstedtgroup.com/pdf/T_D_Magazine_secondlife_article_07.pdf

Habbo Hotel (2011). What is Habbo Hotel? Retrieved from www.habbo.com/groups/officialparentsguide

Hall, T., & Nguyen, F. (2007). IBM@Play on Second Life. *Training Media Review,* July, 2007.

Keegan, Victor (2010, August 21). Virtual worlds: Is this where real life is heading? *The Observer.* Retrieved from www.theguardian.com/technology/2010/aug/22/discover-virtual-worlds-revolution

Kemp, J., & Livingstone, D. (2006). Putting a second life "metaverse" skin on learning management systems. Retrieved from http://cmapsconverted.ihmc.us/rid=1166848858687_1820623091_2414/whitepaper.pdf

Kzero (2011, February 11). VW registered accounts for Q1 2011 reach 1.185bn. Retrieved from www.kzero.co.uk/blog//vw-registered-accounts-for-q1-2011-reach-1-185bn

Lamb, G. M. (2006, October 5). Real learning in a virtual world. *Christian Science Monitor.* Retrieved from www.csmonitor.com/2006/1005/p13s02-legn.html

Linden, P. (2006, July 27). Immersive archeology—Aura Lily breathes life into the architecture and culture of ancient Egypt. *Flickr.* Retrieved from www.flickr.com/photos/pathfinderlinden/199856708/in/set-72157594214266172

Linden Lab. (2011). About Second Life. Retrieved from http://lindenlab.com/about

Linden Lab. (2013a, June 20). Infographic: 10 years of Second Life. Retrieved from http://lindenlab.com/releases/infographic-10-years-of-second-life

Linden Lab. (2013b). Second education directory: Academic organizations in Second Life. Retrieved from www.wiki.secondlife.com/wiki/Second_Life_Education Directory

Magid, L. (2009, February 11). Learning architecture in a virtual world. *CBS News.* Retrieved from www.cbsnews.com/ 2100-500163_162-3271133.html

Mollman, S. (2007, September 23). Second Life's 2nd value: Testing ideas. *CNN.com/World Business.* Retrieved from http://edition.cnn.com/2007/BUSINESS/09/16/second.life

Mosher, B. (2004, July 1). The power of informal learning. Retrieved from http://clomedia.com/articles/view/the_power_of_informal_learning

New Business Horizons. (2011). Companies and organisations in Second Life—Portal. Retrieved from www.nbhorizons.com/list.htm

Newswire Today. (2007, June 26). Functional applications in Second Life—Teamwork training simulation. Retrieved from www.newswiretoday.com/news/20187

Nolan, R. B. (2006, September 27). At law school, 'Second Life' in the cards, and the course catalogue. *The Harvard Crimson*. Retrieved from www.thecrimson.com/article/2006/9/27/at-law-school-second-life-in

Ondrejka, C. (2007, Summer). Collapsing geography: Second Life, innovation, and the future of national power. Innovations case narrative: Second Life. *Innovations, 2*(3), 27–54. Retrieved from www.mitpressjournals.org/doi/pdf/10.1162/itgg.2007.2.3.27

Science Daily (2008, July 21). Second Life improves real-life social skills. Retrieved from www.sciencedaily.com/releases/2008/07/080717210838.htm

Sheehy, P. (2009a,December 22). The immigrant experience. Retrieved from http://ramapoislands.edublogs.org/2009/12/22/the-immigration-experience

Sheehy, P. (2009b, June 5). When the planets align… or not. Retrieved from http://ramapoislands.edublogs.org/2009/06/05/when-the-planets-alignor-not/#more-150

Sheehy, P. (2011, March). As the worldz turn—Presentation transcript. Retrieved from http://ramapoislands.edublogs.org/where-have-i-been

Terdiman, D. (2005, April 6). Second life teaches life lessons. *Wired Magazine*. Retrieved from www.wired.com/gaming/gamingreviews/news/2005/04/67142

Virtual Macbeth. (2011). Foul whisperings, strange matters—A Second Life treatment of Macbeth. Retrieved from http://virtualmacbeth.wikispaces.com

Wallace, M. (2006, August 20). Mitch Kapor on the power of Second Life. 3pointD.com: The Metaverse and 3D Web, as blogged by Mark Wallace and friends. Retrieved from www.3pointd.com/20060820/mitch-kapor-on-the-power-of-second-life

WiloStar3D. (2011). How Avatar Storytellers works. Avatar Storytellers: K–12 Virtual Worlds. Retrieved from www.avatarstorytellers.com/default.asp?iId=GDHJMI

Vassar College. (2007). Vassar's virtual Sistine Chapel. Retrieved from www.vassar.edu/headlines/2007/sistine-chapel.html

Young, J. R. (2010, February 14). After frustrations in Second Life, colleges look to new virtual worlds. *The Chronicle of Higher Education*. Retrieved from http://chronicle.com/article/After-Frustrations-in-Second/64137

CHAPTER 4

K–12 Online Learning
A Worldwide Perspective

Michael Barbour and Kathryn Kennedy

K–12 ONLINE LEARNING is often used as an umbrella term to describe all instances of kindergarten through Grade 12 students' learning by using the Internet. This chapter will explore the state of K–12 online learning in North America and around the world. From correspondence education to complete online schools that are found in some school districts today, K–12 online learning is continuing to grow at seemingly exponential rates. Policies in various districts and countries, along with the individual needs of students and goals for the education system, have often dictated—or at least influenced—this development. In this chapter, we explore these developments in the United States, Canada, Mexico, Australia, New Zealand, Singapore, South Korea, and Turkey.

K–12 online learning is continuing to grow in the United States. In 2010, there were 450,000 student enrollments in states' virtual schools and more than 2 million in online learning courses; additionally, all 50 states and the District of Columbia offered some form of online learning to their K–12 students (Watson, Murin, Vashaw, Gemin, & Rapp, 2012). Eighty percent of school districts around the United States offer online learning opportunities to K–12 students, and 50% of districts are exploring ways to start home-grown online learning initiatives (Watson, Murin, Vashaw, Gemin, & Rapp, 2010). Described as a way to learn anywhere at any time, K–12 online learning has grown significantly as a viable educational choice, often because cyber charter schools have been marketed either as a school choice or as an alternative for homeschooling students. In fact, a recent prediction claims online learning will encompass half of U.S. K–12 education by the year 2020 (Christensen, Johnson, & Horn, 2011).

The K–12 online learning phenomenon is not exclusive to the United States. In a 2009 interview with *THE Journal: Transforming Education Through Technology,* President of the International Association for K–12 Online Learning (iNACOL) Susan Patrick explained that many countries were blazing trails for K–12 online learning. Since 2003, Mexico has trained its preservice teachers to teach online and to use digital content to enhance learning environments, and China is following in Mexico's footsteps (Nagel, 2009). Approximately 5% of all K–12 students in Canada have access to online learning (Barbour, 2012). In Singapore, 100% of teachers are trained to teach online. In Australia, New South Wales is harnessing K–12 online learning by offering students in remote and isolated places a chance to take courses to which students in the more populated areas have direct access (Powell, 2008). Later in this chapter, additional countries' online programs will be highlighted.

The rest of this chapter outlines the growth of K–12 online learning and discusses current developments in online education. Definitions used in the field of K–12 online learning will be demystified, and models of virtual schools will be presented in the first section of this chapter. Then, the current state of virtual schooling in the United States will be shared, followed by a discussion of K–12 online learning activities in Canada and Mexico. Finally, we will end with a discussion of K–12 online learning in countries outside North America, with specific information on Australia, New Zealand, Singapore, South Korea, and Turkey.

Virtual Schools, Cyber Schools— What's the Difference?

Words used in the field of K–12 online learning are abundant and confusing at times, especially when media and practitioners use them interchangeably. To demystify this collection of terminology, we have consulted various sources to distinguish between one term and another. The terms that will be defined here include brick-and-mortar school, virtual school, cyber school, blended learning and blended programs, hybrid learning and hybrid programs, and online learning programs.

Terminology, Getting it Straight

A brick-and-mortar school is one that is traditional, where students and teachers are in a physical classroom, learning in that classroom is based on a set schedule, and 100% of learning is done in a face-to-face (teacher-to-students) format (Allen & Seaman, 2010). Virtual schools are typically supplemental (i.e., not full-time) entities, meaning the K–12 students who take online classes from virtual schools are also enrolled in a brick-and-mortar school. In most instances, these students spend the majority of their time in a traditional classroom and take one or two online courses from the virtual school—often because these courses are not available at their school, they conflict with the timetable for their other courses, or the students have not had successful learning experiences in these courses or subject areas in their traditional classroom environments. Further, in many instances virtual schools do not grant credit to students but forward students' results on to the students' brick-and-mortar schools, and then these schools grant the students credit on their permanent records. Essentially, the virtual and traditional schools work together to educate students. In contrast, cyber schools typically run full-time programs, offering students 100% of their coursework online (Barbour, 2009a).

Blended and hybrid are two terms that are thought by many to be synonymous. For example, Allen and Seaman (2010) combine the words to from one classification: "… 30–79%—Blended/Hybrid—course that blends online and face-to-face delivery. Substantial proportion of the content is delivered online, typically uses online discussions, and typically has some face-to-face meetings" (p. 4). We, however, think these terms need to be differentiated in the following ways. Hybrid refers to cyber schools that might have a face-to-face component. In hybrid models, online learning occurs separately from face-to-face learning. An example of a hybrid school would be Odyssey Charter School in Las Vegas, Nevada. At Odyssey, students are physically present in the school for only one morning or one afternoon a week to take one course in a face-to-face fashion; then they meet with their online teachers. Odyssey students take all their other courses online (Barbour & Plough, 2009). However, in hybrid schools, all of the students' courses come from a single entity or school.

Blended models take place when students attend a brick-and-mortar school and are present in classrooms where they take face-to-face courses from teachers and may sometimes meet one-on-one with teachers. They also engage in online learning components while they are in the classrooms. An example of this would be Voise Academy in Chicago. At Voise, the students are in face-to-face courses that are enhanced by online curriculum elements. Teachers at this school are facilitators of the students' learning and are in charge of providing one-on-one instruction as needed (Sloan & Mackey, 2009). Blended learning could be considered Allen and Seaman's (2010) web-facilitated classification, for which 1% to 29% of the course uses technology on the Internet to enhance what is done in the face-to-face learning environment (although Allen and Seaman's specific percentages do not apply to other blended models). In some cases, the online component is where the syllabus and course schedule are posted and where assignments are submitted into a face-to-face course or learning management system.

The terms hybrid and blended can also be used to describe programs, so a hybrid program is one that offers a buffet of face-to-face and online courses that are separate from one another. Blended programs offer students a face-to-face traditional classroom with online learning opportunities during that classroom time. Both blended and hybrid courses offer online course content, online instruction, digital/adaptive curricula or software, and course management systems.

Defining Models of K–12 Online Learning Programs

There are various models that further distinguish existing K–12 online learning programs. Table 4.1 describes and provides examples of each of these models.

TABLE 4.1 ▶ Categories of K–12 online learning programs (Table 4.1 is adapted from Watson, Winograd, and Kalmon's (2004) six categories of virtual schools, p. 427.)

TYPE OF VIRTUAL SCHOOL	DESCRIPTION	EXAMPLES
Statewide supplemental programs	Students take individual courses from supplemental programs while attending a physical school or cyber school within the state for their main coursework. These programs are authorized by the state and overseen by state education governing agencies.	Michigan Virtual School, Idaho Digital Learning Academy
Single-district schools	These schools provide an alternative to the traditional face-to-face school environment and are offered by individual districts for students within that district who need individualized programs. Alternative schools offer online courses, face-to-face courses, one-on-one tutoring, and counseling as needed. These schools are typically operated by autonomous districts and are generally not tracked by state agencies.	Riverside (CA), Broward (FL), Plano (TX), Los Angeles (CA), JeffCo (CO), WOLF (NV)
Multi-district schools	These schools are operated within individual school districts but enroll students from other school districts within the state. This represents the largest growth sector in K–12 online learning. Multidistrict schools offer online and hybrid courses.	Oregon Connections Academy, Insight School of Washington
Cyber charters	These schools are chartered within a single district but can draw students from across the state. In many cases, they are connected in some way to commercial curriculum providers. Cyber charters offer fully online and hybrid courses.	Georgia Virtual Academy, Minnesota Virtual High School
Consortium	These are supplemental programs that can be statewide, national, or global.	Virtual High School Global Consortium, Wisconsin eSchool Network, Oregon Virtual Education Center (ORVED)
Post-secondary	These programs are run by universities and colleges and offer both supplemental and full-time options for K–12 students. They typically offer their services nationally. Most courses are fully online; some may be hybrid.	University of Nebraska Independent Study High School, Brigham Young University—Independent Study

It is important to note that there are exceptions to each of these types of K–12 online learning programs. There are a few main continuums that are used to classify K–12 online learning programs that are outlined well in the annual *Keeping Pace with K–12 Online Learning* reports (Watson et al., 2010).

Comprehensiveness is a term used to distinguish whether a school or district offers supplemental and/or full-time online options to students. If the school offers supplemental programs, then typically, the students who take its courses are home schooled and/or attending a brick-and-mortar school. States require K–12 online learning programs that offer students full-time options to abide by the same accountability standards as their brick-and-mortar counterparts.

Another term used to distinguish among K–12 online learning programs is "reach," which helps explain where the school operates (i.e., in a school, school district, various school districts, or state). Some programs even venture to offer their programs nationally and internationally (Watson et al., 2010). Whether the course is delivered in real time or not (i.e., synchronous vs. asynchronous) is another distinction that is typically made when considering K–12 online learning programs. For instance, some programs might require a frequent same-time chat or web conference where all students and the teacher meet in a virtual class, chat, or web conference room to discuss content. Other programs might not be able to offer same-/real-time interactions since students and teachers might have conflicting schedules, so teachers' lectures and students' discussions might be uploaded and observed by students at their convenience.

Some programs offer blended or hybrid options on a continuum that spans from 100% online to 100% face-to-face. In addition to these terms, other continuums offer some definitions for particular K–12 online learning programs. For example, what roles teachers play form important distinctions: do teachers lead instruction, support learning, or are they involved in the students' learning at all? Along similar lines, students' roles make distinctions: Are students being provided only teacher-driven learning? Is students' learning being guided to any extent by the teacher? Or are students learning independently? Another continuum would be to look at the levels of student support offered by the program: are students offered little-to-no support, support via a mentor at a school, or support at home and at school?

State of K–12 Online Learning in the United States

The Past

U.S. K–12 distance education has undergone continual change. K–12 online learning originated with correspondence (via U.S. mail on paper) distance education courses offered by the University of Chicago beginning in 1891 (Greenway & Vanourek, 2006). From correspondence mail to radio to television to computers and the Internet, emerging technological innovations have changed the education landscape (Clark, 2007). Laurel Springs Preparatory High School started in 1991, and by 1994, it was recognized as one of the first schools in the United States to offer a comprehensive online curriculum (Laurel Springs School, 2011).

By the mid- to late 1990s, statewide programs had begun. Due to Utah's school shortage and ever-expanding K–12 population, Governor Michael Levitt established Utah's Electronic High School (EHS) (Center for Educational Leadership and Technology, 2008). The first U.S. statewide virtual high school, EHS offers a curriculum that supplements traditional brick-and-mortar coursework and is asynchronous, allowing for independent study and self-pacing. EHS students also have an open-entry/open-exit option, allowing them to start and end a course whenever they want. They are not tied to an academic calendar.

Florida Virtual School (FLVS) began as Florida High School in 1997 as a joint effort between the Orange and Alachua county school districts with an allocation of $200,000 from the state legislature (Friend & Johnston, 2005). Initially, and to this day, FLVS's mission is to serve students statewide. As of 1999, FLVS was "funded through a legislative line item appropriation to the State Department of Education" (Clark, 2001, p. 5). However, in 2001 FLVS became its own school district and is currently funded using the same full-time equivalency formula used for Florida's brick-and-mortar schools. Under this model, money is allocated to school districts (including FLVS) based on where students choose to enroll. During its first year of operation, FLVS enrolled 77 students. In 2011–2012, FLVS's enrollment was 314,593 (www.flvs.net/areas/aboutus/Documents/2013_FLVS_Policy_Brief.pdf).

The Virtual High School (VHS) Global Consortium was created as the Concord Virtual School in Massachusetts in fall 1997 by way of a five-year, $7.4 million federal grant called Stars Initiative (Pape, Adams, & Ribeiro, 2005). The Concord VS was administered by the Hudson Public Schools and the Concord Consortium (Clark, 2001). The VHS Global Consortium is a cooperative high school that develops its own courses internally. The VHS Consortium includes schools that become affiliates to create and offer courses for VHS; affiliate schools pay a fee for their participation in the consortium. Affiliates cover their participation fees by charging students enrollment fees. More than 575 schools are members of the VHS Global Consortium with students from 30+ states and 20+ countries. Cooperating schools may choose from over 140 online courses furnished by the consortium (Pape, 2009). The VHS Consortium's growth rate has been increasing from 10% to 25% per year, and, as of 2010, it had 12,893 enrollments internationally (Watson et al., 2010). VHS, FLVS and Utah's EHS positioned themselves as the early pioneers of K–12 online learning (Clark, 2007).

The Present

The *Keeping Pace with K–12 Online Learning* report, published annually, offers an overview of K–12 virtual schooling in the United States. According to the 2013 report, all 50 states and the District of Columbia offer K–12 students some form of online learning. Twenty six of those states have a state-led online learning initiative or state virtual school. Thirty states in addition to the District of Columbia have a full-time online school option for their K–12 students. One of the fastest growing trends in the K–12 online learning arena is the development of K–12 online learning programs at the individual district level; many of these district-level programs are combining the best of the brick-and-mortar classrooms and online learning to offer their students blended and hybrid opportunities.

A look at each state provides more details regarding K–12 online learning (See Table 4.2).

TABLE 4.2 ▶ **Supplemental and full-time K–12 online learning activities by state** (adapted from the 2013 edition of *Keeping Pace with K–12 Online Learning*)

K–12 ONLINE LEARNING PROGRAMS OFFERED					
	Supplemental			Full-time		
STATE	9–12	6–8	K–5	9–12	6–8	K–5
Alabama	Most	Some	None or few	None or few	None or few	None or few
Alaska	Some	Some	None or few	Some	Some	Some
Arizona	Most	Some	Some	All	All	All
Arkansas	Some	None or few	None or few	Some	Some	None or few
California	Some	Some	None or few	Most	Most	Most
Colorado	Some	None or few	None or few	All	All	All
Connecticut	Some	None or few	None or few	None or few	None or few	None or few
Delaware	None or few	None or few	None or few	None or few	None or few	None or few
Florida	All	All	All	All	All	All
Georgia	Most	Some	None or few	All	All	All
Hawaii	Most	Some	None or few	None or few	None or few	None or few
Idaho	Most	Some	None or few	All	All	All
Illinois	Some	None or few	None or few	None or few	None or few	None or few
Indiana	Some	None or few	None or few	All	All	All
Iowa	Some	None or few	None or few	Some	Some	Some
Kansas	Most	Most	Some	Most	Most	Most
Kentucky	Some	None or few	None or few	None or few	None or few	None or few
Louisiana	Most	Some	None or few	Most	Most	Most
Maine	Some	None or few	None or few	None or few	None or few	None or few
Maryland	Some	None or few	None or few	None or few	None or few	None or few
Massachusetts	Some	Some	None or few	Some	Some	Some
Michigan	Most	Some	None or few	Most	Some	Some
Minnesota	All	All	Some	All	All	All
Mississippi	Most	None or few	None or few	None or few	None or few	None or few
Missouri	Some	None or few	None or few	None or few	None or few	Some
Montana	Most	Some	None or few	None or few	None or few	None or few
Nebraska	Some	Some	None or few	None or few	None or few	None or few
Nevada	Most	None or few	None or few	All	All	All

(Continued)

TABLE 4.2   ▶   *(Continued)*

	K–12 ONLINE LEARNING PROGRAMS OFFERED					
	Supplemental			Full-time		
STATE	9–12	6–8	K–5	9–12	6–8	K–5
New Hampshire	Most	Some	None or few	Some	Some	None or few
New Jersey	Some	None or few	None or few	None or few	None or few	None or few
New Mexico	Some	Some	None or few	Some	Some	Some
New York	None or few	None or few	Some	None or few	None or few	None or few
North Carolina	Most	Some	None or few	None or few	None or few	None or few
North Dakota	Some	Some	None or few	None or few	None or few	None or few
Ohio	Most	Some	None or few	All	All	All
Oklahoma	Most	None or few	None or few	All	All	All
Oregon	Some	Some	None or few	Most	Most	Most
Pennsylvania	Some	None or few	None or few	All	All	All
Rhode Island	Some	None or few	None or few	None or few	None or few	None or few
South Carolina	Most	None or few	None or few	All	All	All
South Dakota	Most	Some	None or few	None or few	None or few	None or few
Tennessee	None or few	None or few	None or few	None or few	Some	Some
Texas	Some	Some	None or few	Most	Most	Some
Utah	Most	Some	Some	All	All	All
Vermont	Some	Some	None or few	None or few	None or few	None or few
Virginia	Most	Most	Some	None or few	None or few	None or few
Washington	Most	Most	Some	All	All	All
West Virginia	Most	Some	None or few	None or few	None or few	None or few
Wisconsin	Most	Some	None or few	All	All	All
Wyoming	Most	Some	None or few	All	All	All

A number of states have laws requiring students to take an online course before they graduate from high school. For example, Michigan passed legislation in 2006 requiring high school students to have "an online learning experience" before graduating from high school (Watson et al., 2010). According to the Alabama State Department of Education's 2008 mandate, beginning with the 2009–2010 ninth grade student body, all high school students must complete at least one course that is online and/or enhanced by technology in a core or elective track (Cowan, 2009). Further, in 2009, "Graduate New Mexico" was enacted, requiring students to take an advanced placement, distance education, or dual enrollment course to graduate from high school (Watson et al., 2010). Florida mandated that all districts must provide their students with K–12 online learning opportunities, either through their own, homegrown programs or via contract with other state-approved online learning providers.

Additional measures have been enacted to support the growth of K–12 online learning in a number of states. For example, Connecticut passed a law that allows teachers to be certified in any state. That same law also required districts with an 8% or higher dropout rate to create an online credit recovery program to help students catch up and earn enough credits to graduate. Idaho's State Board of Education adopted Standards for Online Teachers. In Wisconsin, teachers have to complete a minimum of 30 hours of professional development before they can teach online. Alabama has started to allow students to earn credits to be considered toward graduation based on mastery rather than accumulating seat time (Watson et al., 2010).

Decreasing budgets and lack of qualified teachers have put considerable pressure on education in general and have prompted more people to think in terms of K–12 online learning. While there is continuous growth of K–12 online learning in the United States, growth is uneven across the states due to various issues. Outdated policies in some states have put a halt to the access and equity of K–12 online learning, including the irrelevant use of seat time measurement; the forced capping of enrollment due to the structure of schools; plus the geographic boundaries from one school, school district, or state to another; and the list goes on.

State of K–12 Online Learning in the Rest of North America

While most of the media attention—and even most of the literature (Barbour, 2009a)—has focused upon K–12 online learning activities in the United States, in many other countries around the world, the provision of K–12 distance education has evolved into extensive online programs for the same number of years as we have had them in the United States. As we considered the two other North American countries, we saw that K–12 online learning in Canada is just as old with similar levels of activity as found in the United States. Mexico, considered to be the economically weakest of the three nations, has more extensive measures in place to promote K–12 online learning than those in the United States.

Canada

Similar to other geographically large countries with comparatively sparse populations, Canada has a long history of supporting K–12 distance education. This began with a correspondence school in British Columbia in 1919, with 86 students (13 of whom were living in lighthouses along the coast) and eventually grew to serve more than 600 students within the first decade (Dunae, 2006). In 1993, British Columbia again led the country with the introduction of two K–12 online learning programs, New Directions in Distance Learning and the EBUS Academy (Dallas, 1999). Other provinces, such as Manitoba, Ontario, Alberta, and Newfoundland and Labrador, followed suit with district-based online programs of their own (Barker & Wendel, 2001; Barker, Wendel, & Richmond, 1999; Haughey & Fenwich, 1996; Stevens, 1997).

Shortly thereafter, Wynne (1997) conducted a review of K–12 online learning across Canada and found that there were few programs outside British Columbia and Alberta. From this early introduction and initially slow growth, K–12 online learning throughout Canada has grown steadily over the past two decades. For example, the Canadian Teachers Federation (2000) estimated that there were approximately 25,000 students enrolled in K–12 online courses. Further, in a study of how schools were using information and communication technologies in Canadian schools, Plante and Beattie (2004) found that almost 30% of all schools and almost 40% of secondary schools in the country were using the Internet for online learning.

In the second annual *State of the Nation: K–12 Online Learning in Canada* report, Barbour (2009b) reported that all 13 provinces and territories had K–12 distance education activity, with British Columbia having the highest number and percentage of participating students and Prince Edward Island having the fewest. The growth focused on providing opportunities to students living in rural jurisdictions. For example, the Canadian Council on Learning (2009) reported that more rural schools than urban schools had students participate in online courses, often in a supplemental manner when courses could not be offered due to limited resources or teachers. In fact, K–12 distance education had historically been viewed as a substitute for face-to-face learning when opportunities were not available to students in other formats (i.e., the belief that face-to-face was the preferred delivery model when it was available)—although that perception is beginning to change as K–12 online learning continues to grow in numbers and in geographic reach.

Barbour (2013), in the most recent annual *State of the Nation: K–12 Online Learning in Canada* report, estimated approximately 245,000 students (or approximately 5% of the total K–12 student population) were enrolled in K–12 distance education programs in Canada, which is similar to the proportion of K–12 students engaged in online learning in the United States. A closer look at the development of K–12 online learning in three of the Canadian provinces, British Columbia, Alberta, and Newfoundland and Labrador, provides an interesting examination of the many different ways these programs have developed.

In British Columbia, the first Canadian province to offer K–12 online learning opportunities, distance education developed in three distinct phases: (1) the correspondence education operated by the Ministry of Education from 1919 until the 1980s, (2) a more decentralized model using regional distance education schools until the mid-1990s, and then (3) the creation of numerous district-based programs heavily regulated by the Ministry of Education for the past decade (Winkelmans, Anderson, & Barbour, 2010). British Columbia is the most heavily regulated jurisdiction in Canada, with legislation creating a quantitative and qualitative audit system to ensure high-quality learning opportunities for K–12 students. Also of note is that the Ministry of Education has created a detailed formula ensuring that the per student funding follows the student, with brick-and-mortar schools receiving some compensation to allow for local support of those students enrolled in distance education opportunities. Three years ago, British Columbia had the highest proportion of students enrolled in K–12 online learning programs, with 78,650 students enrolled in one or more courses during the 2011–2012 school year or 12% of all students (Barbour, 2013).

K–12 online learning in Alberta, on the other hand, developed from a series of district-based programs beginning with a strong, province-wide program that maintained substantial student enrollments. In addition to the differences between the nature of programs that developed in Alberta and British Columbia, even more differences can be noted in how the two provinces regulate K–12 distance education. Unlike British Columbia—where the Ministry of Education had direct involvement, followed by a "hands-on" approach, and then extensive regulations—Alberta has taken an almost completely "hands off" approach. In Alberta's 2009 annual *Guide to Education,* the Ministry advises school districts to consider the following:

> how student attendance is to be defined; the role of parents in instruction, assessment and supervision of student work; staffing levels; time frames for student access to the instructional expertise of teachers; student evaluation practices; requirements for program access by students living outside Alberta; program decisions; e.g., self-paced or teacher controlled, synchronous or asynchronous; how to deliver all outcomes of Alberta programs of study; provision for writing achievement tests and diploma examinations; program and teacher evaluation; how to provide alternative forms of program delivery for non-resident students who are experiencing difficulty in the online environment. (Government of Alberta, 2009, p. 65)

Interestingly, one year later, Alberta's Ministry released the *Inspiring Action on Education* discussion paper, which calls for an education system where teachers can teach in "face-to-face, online, and other non-traditional environments" (Government of Alberta, 2010, p. 24). This vision would essentially create a school system where students, teachers, and administrators are all comfortable with education being delivered with or without technology through a variety of delivery methods.

In contrast with the examples from British Columbia and Alberta, where programs developed primarily into district-based initiatives, Newfoundland and Labrador began with limited, district-based programs, and a combination of the two systems evolved into a single, province-wide virtual school (Barbour, 2005). First, the province started using telematic or audiographic systems that used bridging technology to provide conference calling facilities, including a device that reproduced writing from the teacher's tablet to computer screens linked to the audiographics network (Brown, Sheppard, & Stevens, 2000). Less than a decade later, several district-based online learning programs developed (e.g., East–West Project, Vista School District Digital Intranet, Centre for Advanced Placement Education) providing a model for additional online learning programs. By 2000, the lessons learned from the initial province-wide telematics system, along with the district-based online learning programs, were combined to create a single, province-wide Centre for Distance Learning and Innovation (Sparkes & Williams, 2000).

These three provinces demonstrate the unique nature of the development of K–12 online learning in Canada. Some jurisdictions had long histories with K–12 distance education prior to the development of online learning programs, while others started more recently. Further, some provinces and territories have single or strong province-wide programs, while other jurisdictions have almost exclusively district-based programs. The variety of approaches is largely due to the provincial control over education, as opposed to a system of education that exerts a more centralized or federally controlled education system, such as the one found in Mexico.

Mexico

Mexico is among those countries making giant strides to provide K–12 online learning opportunities. Due to space issues in high schools and colleges, Mexico will have to leverage education using online learning (Barbour, Brown, et al., 2011). According to this 2011 report published by iNACOL, *Online and Blended Learning: A Survey of Policy and Practice of K–12 Schools Around the World,* Mexico has developed government-funded online or blended programs for middle school and high school students. In fact, the report's coauthors report that some form of online learning is available to all students, and blended learning is available to some. An estimated 200,000 students, about 10% of Mexico's middle school and high school student population, attended online schools in 2011. The students came from rural, suburban, and urban areas and from small and large schools. These online learning opportunities continue to provide students additional course options that they might not have access to due to residence in rural locations or these types of courses not being available at their local, traditional schools. Courses are also offered to homebound students on medical leave of absence or those who have special needs. In addition, for migrant workers who need to support their families while away from home and/or who travel often, online learning is ideal. In addition, online learning helps to challenge gifted students, those who want to prepare for colleges using AP courses or college-preparatory courses, and those who want to begin taking college-level courses.

As of 2011, Mexico had at least nine distance education high schools (Barbour, Brown, et al., 2011). These programs, which developed from former *telesecundaria* or television-based programs, are generally operated by universities and focus on rural areas that are unable to support high school teachers (Barbour, 2009a). The main focus of these distance education programs is to help adults finish high school. As Internet access is not available in many portions of the country, particularly in rural areas, many distance education schools still use educational radio, satellite delivery, DVDs, online media, mobile phones, and correspondence coursework via the postal service to facilitate learning. In 2003, Mexico introduced the Enciclomedia program, which digitized K–12 academic content and provided students with online access and CD-access to learning in every school, library, and community technology center (Secretaría de Educación Básica, 2010). Enciclomedia offers technical support, audiovisual representations of curriculum for students, and tutorials that show teachers how to incorporate the Enciclomedia resource into their classes. The teachers' materials are broken down by discipline, in addition to an educational planning series that offers 14 programs. The Latinoamerican Institute for Educational Communication, the Directorate General of Educational Television, and the Directorate General of Educational Materials helped construct these programs. For those interested in creating a resource like Enciclomedia, its site offers a section where the coordinators and founders of this resource discuss the program's purpose and creation along with an overview of how Enciclomedia is positively changing teaching and learning in Mexico (www.sep.gob.mx/en/sep_en/Enciclomedia_program).

By 2004, Mexico mandated that all preservice teachers be trained to teach more effectively by integrating digital content into their curricula (Dawley, 2010). Using Enciclomedia student resources and practical examples, teachers find digital content at their fingertips. In addition, every new teacher was provided a laptop by 2005 (Gillis, Patrick, Reed, Revenaugh, & Watson, 2009). Mexico's universities and colleges are responsible for training K–12 teachers to prepare for online learning and technology integration, and teachers of online courses have no licensing requirements. Mexico is struggling with a lack of policy or policy barriers in terms of access limitations for students who want to take online courses. Funding for professional development and teacher training also is lacking. Despite these roadblocks, Mexico's online learning growth of approximately 15% per year demonstrates this country's robust emergence into the K–12 online learning arena (Barbour, 2013).

State of K–12 Online Learning in the Rest of the World

In 2006, the International Association for K–12 Online Learning (iNACOL) conducted a worldwide survey of approximately 30 departments of education and received responses from 15 countries. In the introduction to its findings, iNACOL wrote, "Research has been done on several virtual schools in North America; however, little information is available about current K–12 e-learning initiatives across the world" (Powell & Patrick, 2006, p. 1). While the situation has changed to some extent in recent years, detailed information on K–12 online learning programs outside North America are lacking. However, Barbour (2009a) noted that "the organization of online learning programs into single entities or schools that provide supplemental or full-time online studies [was] largely a North American phenomenon" (p. 10) which is still largely true.

Based on the 15 responses iNACOL received from its 2006 survey, the levels and scope of virtual schooling outside North America varied significantly. For example, while fewer than 1% of students in China took an online course, the Chinese Ministry of Education planned to reach 100 million more students through online learning over the next 10 years (Barbour, 2010b). India has a similar 10-year goal of universal access to K–12 education, which would require the construction of 200,000 additional schools unless the government focuses its rural endeavors toward online learning. Other countries have chosen a more blended approached, such as Iran, where online courses are developed free of charge and classroom-based teachers are able to use that content as a supplement to their own instruction and curriculum resources. In the United Kingdom, K–12 online learning has been used as a way to extend the traditional classroom to provide students and parents access to curricular materials, instruction, and even student information systems beyond the confines of the regular school day (Harris, 2005).

K–12 online learning activities have been described in several other countries, including Australia, Denmark, France, Iceland, and Sweden (Harris, 2005); Hong Kong, Japan, Kazakhstan, Nepal, New Zealand, Singapore, Tanzania, Turkey, and Zimbabwe (Powell & Patrick, 2006); and Finland and South Korea (Barbour, 2010b). The following sections describe the development and situations of K–12 online learning activities in five of these countries: Australia, New Zealand, Singapore, South Korea, and Turkey.

Australia

The use of distance education at all K–12 levels is not new across Australia. More than 60 years ago, the first School of the Air was established, using educational radio as a way to provide opportunities to rural students—and there were still 20 of these distance education programs operating in the late 1990s (Moore & Kearsley, 1996). Virtual schooling has also developed extensively in recent years. Powell and Patrick (2006) describe the development of the Country's Areas Program (CAP), which provides online learning opportunities to rural students in the New South Wales region, reporting that the "CAP works with the state's Distance Education Centers to share resources and lessons. The Distance Education Centers provide video satellite feeds to students to provide synchronous collaborations amongst students and their teachers to create a blended learning environment" (para. 6).

As well as the CAP, New South Wales offers additional K–12 online learning. Harris (2008) described the Northern Beaches Christian School (NBCS), which offers online learning in partnership with the Sydney Centre for Innovation in Learning. In 2001, the NBCS first developed a school portal and course management system to allow classroom-based teachers the opportunity to use online resources and instruction in their face-to-face teaching. This was followed in 2006 by the development and delivery of completely online courses, with an initial enrollment of 15 students from four schools and grew to more than 200 students in 40 schools only two years later (Harris, 2008).

Beyond the online programs available in New South Wales, Barbour (2010b) reported the existence of the Virtual School for the Gifted and the Virtual Schooling Service in Australia. Barbour's conference paper's focus on programs in New South Wales may have been a reflection of the specific individuals who completed the iNACOL survey and the limited literature in K–12 online learning—particularly given Australia's long history with the Schools of the Air and the fact that telematics had been used at the K–12 level since the late 1970s or early 1980s (Oliver & Reeves, 1994).

New Zealand

The use of distance learning throughout K–12 education began in New Zealand around 1922, with the introduction of the Correspondence School (Barbour & Wenmoth, 2013). While the Correspondence School continues to offer K–12 distance education opportunities using the traditional postal mail system, beginning in 1994—with the CANTAtech project—the use of Internet-based distance education has increased steadily. This increasing development of K–12 virtual learning in New Zealand schools has focused predominantly on regional and rural settings, as a means of providing access to curricula that schools are unable to offer due to small student enrollment and difficulty in attracting and retaining teachers in specialized subject areas (Wenmoth, 1996).

In 2002, the first regional network or cluster in New Zealand began connecting its classes using videoconferencing. The following year, the Virtual Learning Network (VLN)—essentially a national virtual school—was established. The primary focus of the VLN was to broker a model for sharing videoconferencing courses among K–12 schools and these regional clusters (Barbour, 2011). In 2004, the Ministry of Education published a handbook to assist schools in forming virtual learning clusters. *Learning Communities Online: A Handbook for Schools (LCO Handbook)* contained a matrix to guide development from initial conception to implementation. The matrix included areas such as relationships and communication, logistical coordination, student needs, staffing and professional development, technical coordination, learning resources, and others focused on how to introduce virtual learning into the school and establish the administrative supports that were needed.

The number of clusters and schools involved with the VLN has grown significantly in recent years. In addition, schools in urban areas have been taking advantage of opportunities for collaboration, including curriculum and resource sharing with the help of Ultra-Fast Broadband. In 2009, more than 20 of these clusters existed (Compton, Davis, & Mackey, 2009), representing 1401 student enrollments from 252 schools in 212 different courses taught by 154 distance or e-teachers (Roberts, 2009). The *LCO Handbook* has been extensively revised with an additional dimension added to the matrix to address issues of sustainability and maturity. While the first edition of the handbook focused on assisting schools with becoming involved with the VLN and the initial creation of regional clusters, the updated handbook places a greater emphasis on strategies and tools that participating schools and clusters can use to sustain and expand their involvement with the VLN. The *LCO Handbook* was made available in February 2011, by CORE Education Ltd. and the New Zealand Ministry of Education (www.vln.school.nz). (For additional information on New Zealand's technology in education programs, see www.minedu.govt.nz/theministry/educationinitiatives/ufbinschools.aspx & www.med.govt.nz/sectors-industries/technology-communication/fast-broadband/education)

Singapore

According to Powell and Patrick (2006) K–12 schools have the ability to determine the method used to integrate information technology. In Singapore, the national goal mandated that all secondary schools (i.e., Grades 7–10) and junior colleges (i.e., Grades 11 and 12) have a course management system by the end of 2006. As of May 2006, all secondary schools and junior colleges, along with 85% of primary schools (Grades 1– 6) were using course management systems. While this allowed for almost all K–12 students throughout the country to be able to take an online learning course, Powell and Patrick indicated that the blended approach is often used, combining a mixture of face-to-face instruction with online learning in the classroom environment.

The pervasive infrastructure in place that allows K–12 online learning has also enabled the system to shut down and use online learning as a part of its pandemic drills. Powell and Patrick describe this as follows:

> a number of schools in Singapore have adopted e-Learning week, where students do not attend school but stay at home working on lessons and assignments delivered through the learning management system. During this week, teachers facilitate the learning and provide feedback via email and other electronic means. (p. 20)

These e-learning weeks have continued to grow in size, with more schools, teachers, and students participating each year.

The growth of K–12 online learning and participation in the annual e-learning weeks has been supported by the national teacher education program, which has provided preservice and in-service teachers with initial training and ongoing professional development into online course design and online pedagogy. In 2006, the government provided $500 million to fund research designed to support "Singapore's long-term vision of growing into a global interactive and digital media capital that will fully leverage the Web 2.0 space" (Koh & Lee, 2008, p. 89). As Powell (2010) reported, the Ministry of Education in Singapore wanted "to take education into the next generation of technologies and pedagogical practices by prototyping and studying educational gaming, virtual worlds for learning such as Second Life" (p. 77). These measures were designed to place Singapore at the forefront of digital education worldwide.

South Korea

From 1996 to 2011, the South Korea central government implemented three Master Plans related to the use of information and communications technologies (ICT) in education. From 1996 to 2000, Master Plan I put computers and Internet access in Korean classrooms and provided initial ICT literacy. Master Plan II, from 2001 to 2005, first saw online course content development and distribution, along with teacher training. This was followed by the creation or reorganization of specific K–12 e-learning programs (e.g., Cyber Home Learning System [CHLS] and EBS video streaming). From 2006 to 2011, Master Plan III focused on extending these programs, as well as exploring mobile learning research and development opportunities (Korean Education and Research Information Service, 2008).

One of the main driving forces behind the growth of K–12 online learning and the CHLS has been student aspirations for a post-secondary education. More than 80% of Korean students attend colleges or universities (Song & Kim, 2009). Competition for entrance into the best-ranked colleges and universities requires that parents purchase additional tutoring beyond formal schooling; in some instances the cost of this additional private tutoring can be the single biggest household expense for many families. The CHLS provides supplemental learning opportunities to reduce the cost of this private tutoring and eliminate the gap between regions and classes. The CHLS has grown significantly. For example, in 2005 there were approximately 750,000 students who had registered with the CHLS. By 2008, the government-run CHLS was being used by 3.09 million students, with an 86% increase in the number of classes and a 100% increase in the number of students per class from the previous year (Korean Education and Research Information Service, 2009). Approximately 10,000 teachers were working as cyber tutors as of 2008, serving students in pedagogical, administrative, social, and technical roles (Bae, Han, Lee, & Lee, 2008). One of the successes of the CHLS programs is that over one third of registered users stopped or planned to stop paying to use the private tutor system. Even more recently, Korea Education and Research Information Service (2011) found that there were over four million users of the CHLS, with more than 200,000 of those users logging into the system each day.

Turkey

Similar to South Korea, the need for K–12 online learning in Turkey is being driven by the state's mandated testing. Students in Grades 6, 7, and 8 are required to complete statewide standardized exams in all of their core subject areas. Upon graduating from primary school, it is the students' performances on these exams that determine their secondary school placements.

Such high-stakes testing has precipitated the growth of a private tutoring industry, along with several government initiatives designed to provide similar opportunities to low-income families unable to afford private tutorials (Sakar & Ozturk, 2011). Beyond the provision of online tutoring to K–12 students, several K–12 distance education opportunities have been offered in Turkey, including for vocational education.

Following the success of similar programs in higher education, along with a successful K–12 instructional television program, in 1992, Turkey's Ministry of National Education established an open high school. Based on a correspondence education model (i.e., instructional packages and assessments sent via postal mail), the open high school program began with almost 45,000 students in its first year of operation (Demiray & Adiyaman, 2002). Within five years, the open high school's enrollment had doubled to 90,000 students. By the 2008–2009 school year, about 10 years later, the open school's enrollment was approximately 1.3 million.

According to Powell and Patrick (2006), a new initiative known as the "Online Big Project" began in 2006. A collaboration between the government and a series of non-governmental organizations and private businesses, the goal of the Online Big Project was to provide the entire (K–8) elementary school curriculum in an online format, to be followed by the digitization of the entire secondary school curriculum. At the time, it was expected that the elementary school pilot would service more than 200,000 students during their initial pilot year and more than 11,000,000 within three years of operation.

Summary

Our goal for this chapter was to explore the state of K–12 online learning in the United States, North America, and around the world. K–12 online learning is the umbrella term used to describe all instances of students who are learning using the Internet.

From 1891's correspondence courses to today's fully online, hybrid, and blended learning opportunities, K–12 online learning in the United States is continuing to grow. New statewide policies are making K–12 online learning an integral part of the education system. Trends such as home-grown district-level programs have provided new challenges for educators in terms of what model works best and for whom. With 49 out of 50 states and the District of Columbia offering online learning opportunities to K–12 populations around the country, this sector of education is continuing to see steady growth.

Just over the border to the North and the South, Canada and Mexico have established online learning opportunities that reach their K–12 populations. While Mexico is providing laptops for every teacher and ensuring they can integrate digital content into their curricula, Canada is continuing its growth in online learning by way of district-level and province-wide online programs that are home-grown within provinces. Because Canada's provinces have much more control than U.S. states do, examples of how K–12 online learning has entered the education system in Canada are numerous. In Mexico, on the other hand, the government has a centralized system providing the same opportunities to all students within the country. Both countries are expecting exponential grown in K–12 online learning in the coming years.

Beyond North America, K–12 online learning is booming. Australia reaches students online who have remote access to traditional education opportunities. New Zealand continues to offer correspondence coursework to its K–12 population and has seen a rise in the use of the Internet for content delivery, particularly with the use of videoconferencing. Singapore's government invested funds for the continual professional development of its K–12 teachers, which enables it to harness online pedagogical practices for the overall betterment of the country's education system. South Korea, in hopes to alleviate extensive tutoring fees incurred by families, offers supplemental online learning to K–12 students. And Turkey is building an online learning infrastructure with its Online Big Project initiative with goals reverberating across the entire country.

So what does this chapter say about K–12 online learning? The steady, often exponential growth of this educational opportunity has caused excitement and some growing pains, especially for programs that were started in the early to mid-1990s. Now that some explicit models have been established, programs have effective guidelines to follow, as well as contacts and examples to seek out for advice. Advocates for K–12 online learning are continuing to advocate for policy changes that support effective programs, and as programs grow, practitioners look for practical research that will advance the K–12 online learning field.

References

Allen, I. E., & Seaman, J. (2010). *Learning on demand: Online education in the United States, 2009.* Newburyport, MA: Sloan Consortium. Retrieved from sloanconsortium.org/publications/survey/pdf/learningondemand.pdf

Bae, H., Han, K-W., Lee, E. K., & Lee, Y. J. (2008). The cyber home learning system for primary and secondary schools students in Korea: Current state and challenges. In K. McFerrin et al. (Eds.), *Proceedings of the annual conference of the society for information technology and teacher education* (pp. 2887–2891). Norfolk, VA: Association for the Advancement of Computing in Education (AACE).

Barbour, M. K. (2005). From telematics to web-based: The progression of distance education in Newfoundland and Labrador. *British Journal of Educational Technology, 36*(6), 1055–1058.

Barbour, M. K. (2009b). *State of the nation study: K–12 online learning in Canada.* Vienna, VA: International Association for K–12 Online Learning. Retrieved from www.inacol.org/research/docs/iNACOL_CanadaStudy_200911.pdf

Barbour, M. K. (2010a). *State of the nation study: K–12 online learning in Canada.* Vienna, VA: International Council for K–12 Online Learning. Retrieved from www.inacol.org/research/docs/iNACOL_CanadaStudy10-finalweb.pdf

Barbour, M. K. (2010b). Perspectives on e-learning: Development and challenges of K–12 online learning. In D. Gibson & B. Dodge (Eds.), *Proceedings of the society for information technology & teacher education international conference* (pp. 310–315). Chesapeake, VA: AACE. Retrieved from www.editlib.org/p/33355

Barbour, M. K. (2011). *Primary and secondary e-learning: Examining the process of achieving maturity.* Christchurch, New Zealand: Distance Education Association of New Zealand. Retrieved from www.vln.school.nz/mod/file/download.php?file_guid=114023

Barbour, M. K. (2012). State of the nation: K–12 online learning in Canada. Victoria, BC: Open School BC/Vienna, VA: International Council for K–12 Online Learning. Retrieved from www.openschool.bc.ca/pdfs/iNACOL_CanadaStudy_2012.pdf

Barbour, M. K. (2013). The landscape of K–12 online learning: Examining what is known. In M. G. Moore (Ed.), *Handbook of distance education* (3rd ed., pp. 574–93). New York, NY: Routledge. Retrieved from www.academia.edu/2426553/Barbour_M._K._2013_._The_landscape_of_K-12_online_learning_Examining_what_is_known._In_M._G._Moore_Eds._Handbook_of_distance_education_3rd_ed._pp._574-593_._New_York_Routledge

Barbour, M. K., Brown, R., Waters, L. H., Hoey, R., Hunt, J. L., Kennedy, K., Ounsworth, C., Powell, A., & Trimm, T. (2011). *Online and blended learning: A survey of policy and practice of K–12 schools around the world.* Vienna, VA: International Association for K–12 Online Learning (iNACOL). Retrieved from www.inacol.org/cms/wp-content/uploads/2012/11/iNACOL_IntnlReport2011.pdf

Barbour, M. K., & Plough, C. (2009). Social networking in cyberschooling: Helping to make online learning less isolating. *Tech Trends, 53*(4), 56–60. Retrieved from www.academia.edu/2311550/Barbour_M._K._and_Plough_C._2009_._Social_networking_in_cyberschooling_Helping_to_make_online_learning_less_isolating._Tech_Trends_53_4_56-60

Barbour, M. K., & Stewart, R. (2008). *A snapshot state of the nation study: K–12 online learning in Canada.* Vienna, VA: North American Council for Online Learning (NACOL). Retrieved from www.learningace.com/doc/957552/2d7f6bce0f0df585470fb6fd1d39c58c/nacol_canadastudy-lr

Barbour, M. K., & Wenmoth, D. (2013). Virtual learning as an impetous for educational change: Charting a way forward for learning in New Zealand. Christchurch, New Zealand: CORE Education. Retrieved from www.core-ed.org/sites/core-ed.org/files/VLN_Barbour_Wenmoth-v3a.pdf

Barker, K., & Wendel, T. (2001). *e-Learning: Studying Canada's virtual secondary schools.* Kelowna, BC: Society for the Advancement of Excellence in Education. Retrieved from http://web.archive.org/web/20050311224025/http://www.excellenceineducation.ca/pdfs/006.pdf

Barker, K., Wendel, T., & Richmond, M. (1999). *Linking the literature: School effectiveness and virtual schools.* Vancouver, BC: FuturEd. Retrieved from http://web.archive.org/web/20060527205905/http://www.futured.com/pdf/Virtual.pdf

Brown, J., Sheppard, B., Stevens, K., Boone, W., & Gill, L. (2000). *Effective schooling in a telelearning environment.* St. John's, NL: Centre for TeleLearning and Rural Education. Retrieved from http://web.archive.org/web/20041027051254/www.tellearn.mun.ca/es_report/index.html

Canadian Teachers Federation. (2000). *Fact sheets on contractual issues in distance/online education.* Ottawa, ON: Author.

Canadian Council of Learning. (2009, May). *State of e-learning in Canada.* Ottawa, ON: Author. Retrieved from www.ccl-cca.ca/pdfs/E-learning/E-Learning_Report_FINAL-E.PDF

Center for Educational Leadership and Technology. (2008). *Utah's electronic high school audit report.* Marlborough, MA: Center for Educational Leadership and Technology.

Christensen, C., Johnson, C., & Horn, M. (2011). *Disrupting class, expanded edition: How disruptive innovation will change the way the world learns.* New York, NY: McGraw-Hill.

Clark, T. (2001, October). *Virtual schools: Trends and issues—a study of virtual schools in the United States.* San Francisco, CA: Western Regional Educational Laboratories. Retrieved from www.wested.org/online_pubs/virtualschools.pdf

Clark, T. (2007). Virtual and distance education in North American schools. In M. G. Moore (Ed.), *Handbook of Distance Education* (2nd ed., pp. 473–490). Mahwah, NJ: Lawrence Erlbaum.

Compton, L. K. L., Davis, N., & Mackey, J. (2009, October). Field experience in virtual schools— To be there virtually. *Journal of Technology and Teacher Education, 17*(4), 459–477. Retrieved from www.editlib.org/p/28316

Cowan, K. (2009). Learning across distance: Virtual-instruction programs are growing rapidly, but the impact on "brick-and-mortar" classrooms is still up in the air. *Harvard Education Letter, 25*(1), 2. Retrieved from www.kristinacowan.com/wp-content/uploads/2012/10/Learning-Across-Distance_Harvard-clip-Jan-08.pdf

Dallas, J. (1999). *Distance education for kindergarten to grade 12: A Canadian perspective.* A presentation at the Pan-Commonwealth Forum, Brunei. Retrieved from http://teachingandlearningonline.wikispaces.com/Canadian; with link: www.col.org/forum/PCFpapers/PostWork/dallas.pdf

Dawley, L. (2010, June 29). Research round-up: Online learning, a quick reference on the science behind virtual schooling. *Edutopia.* Retrieved from www.edutopia.org/stw-online-learning-research-roundup

Demiray, U., & Adiyaman, Z. (2002). *A review of the literature on the open high school in Turkey on its tenth anniversary between the years 1992–2002.* Eskisehir, TR: Turkish Republic, Ministry of National Education, General Directorate of Educational Technologies.

Dunae, P. A. (2006). *The homeroom: Correspondence education.* Nanaimo, BC: Malaspina University. Published originally in *The School Record* (Victoria: British Columbia Archives and Records Service, 1992), p. 73; Belle C. Gibson, *Teacher-Builder: The life and work of J. W. Gibson* (Victoria, BC: privately printed, 1961), pp. 101–109. Retrieved from www.mala.bc.ca/homeroom/content/topics/programs/corresp.htm

Friend, B., & Johnston, S. (2005). Florida virtual school: A choice for all students. In Z. L. Berge & T. Clark (Eds.), *Virtual schools: Planning for success* (pp. 97–117). New York, NY: Teachers College Press.

Gillis, L., Patrick, S., Reed, J., Revenaugh, M., & Watson, J. (2009). *How to introduce, sustain, and expand K–12 online learning opportunities in your state.* A presentation for Workshop on 21st century learning: Using technology to nurture minds, save taxpayers money, and build globally competitive leaders. Retrieved from http://web.archive.org/web/20110410000911/http://www.alec.org/Content/ContentFolders/Education/EducationReports/ALEC-iNACOL-Webinar.pdf

Government of Alberta. (2009). *Guide to education.* Edmonton, AB: Queen's Printing for Alberta. Retrieved from http://web.archive.org/web/20081116233450/http://education.alberta.ca/media/832568/guidetoed.pdf

Government of Alberta. (2010, June). *Inspiring action on education.* Edmonton, AB: Queen's Printing for Alberta. Retrieved from http://ideas.education.alberta.ca/media/2905/inspiringaction%20eng.pdf

Government of Alberta. (2011). *Education 101.* Retrieved from http://education.alberta.ca/media/6588420/educator101.pdf

Greenway, R., & Vanourek, G. (2006). The virtual revolution: Understanding online schools. *Education Next, (6)*2 (Spring), 35–44. Retrieved from http://media.hoover.org/sites/default/files/documents/ednext20062_34.pdf

Harris, S. (2005). *Online learning in senior secondary school education: Practice, pedagogy and possibilities.* New South Wales, AU: Sydney Centre for Innovation in Learning (SCIL).

Harris, S. (2008). *ICT innovation transforming the heart of the classroom.* New South Wales, AU: SCIL. Retrieved from http://static.squarespace.com/static/510b86cce4b0f6b4fb690106/t/512eb34be4b0c046ed7a70da/1362015051278/stephen-harris_ict-innovation-transforming-the-heart-of-the-classroom.pdf

Haughey, M., & Fenwick, T. (1996). Issues in forming school district consortia to provide distance education: Lessons from Alberta. *Journal of Distance Education, 11*(1), 51–81. Retrieved from www.jofde.ca/index.php/jde/article/view/242/454

Koh, T. S., & Lee, S. C. (2008). Digital skills and education: Singapore's ICT master planning for the school sector. In S. K. Lee, J. P. Tan, B. Fredrikson, & C. B. Goh (Eds.), *Towards a better world: Education and training for economic development of Singapore since 1965* (pp. 167–190). Washington, DC/Singapore: World Bank/National Institute of Education.

Korean Education and Research Information Service. (2011). *Adapting education to the information age.* Seoul, South Korea: Ministry of Education, Science and Technology. Retrieved from http://english.keris.or.kr/ICSFiles/afieldfile/2009/05/07/Whitepaper2008.pdf

Hwang, D. J., Yang, H.-K., & Kim, H. (n.d.). *E-learning in the Republic of Korea.* Moscow, RF: UNESCO. Retrieved from http://iite.unesco.org/pics/publications/en/files/3214677.pdf

Laurel Springs School. (2013). About us. Ojai, CA: Author. Retrieved from http://laurelsprings.com/aboutus

Nagel, D. (2009, October 29). Q&A: iNACOL's Susan Patrick on trends in eLearning. *THE Journal: Transforming Education Through Technology.* Retrieved from http://thejournal.com/Articles/2009/10/29/Q-A-iNACOLs-Susan-Patrick-on-Trends-in-eLearning.aspx?Page=1

Oliver, R., & Reeves, T. C. (1994). *Telematics in rural education: An investigation of the use of telematics for the delivery of specialist programmes for students in rural schools.* Mount Lawley, AU: InTech Innovations.

Pape, L. (2009, November 20). Virtual high school global consortium: The past, present and future. *Seen Magazine.* Retrieved from www.seenmagazine.us/articles/article-detail/articleid/212/virtual-high-school-global-consortium.aspx

Pape, L., Adams, R., & Ribeiro, C. (2005). The virtual high school: Collaboration and online professional development. In Z. L. Berge & T. Clark (Eds.), *Virtual schools: Planning for success* (pp. 118–132). New York, NY: Teachers College Press.

Plante, J., & Beattie, D. (2004). *Connectivity and ICT integration in Canadian elementary and secondary schools: First results from the information and communications technologies in schools survey, 2003–2004.* Ottawa, ON: Statistics Canada.

Powell, A. (2008). K–12 Online learning: A global perspective. In C. Bonk et al. (Eds.), *Proceedings of the world conference on e-learning in corporate, government, healthcare, and higher education 2008* (pp. 2353–2380). Chesapeake, VA: AACE.

Powell, A. (2010). *A case study of e-learning initiatives in New Zealand's secondary schools.* (Unpublished doctoral dissertation). Pepperdine University, Malibu, CA.

Powell, A., & Patrick, S. (2006). *An international perspective of K–12 online learning: A summary of the 2006 NACOL international e-learning survey.* Vienna, VA: North American Council for Online Learning. Retrieved from http://files.eric.ed.gov/fulltext/ED514433.pdf

Roberts, R. (2009). Video conferencing in distance learning: A New Zealand schools' perspective. *Journal of Distance Learning, 13*(1), 91–107. Retrieved from http://journals.akoaotearoa.ac.nz/index.php/JOFDL/article/viewFile/40/38

Sakar, A. N., & Ozturk, O. (2011). The "community services" course through distance education: Evaluation of primary school students. *Turkish Online Journal of Distance Education, 12* (1, January). Retrieved from http://tojde.anadolu.edu.tr/tojde41/articles/article_11.htm

Song, K.-S., & Kim, S.-H. (2009, March). *E-learning applications to meet the special needs of K–12 education in Korea.* A paper presented at the First International Conference on e-Learning and Distance Learning, Riyadh, SA. Retrieved from http://ipac.kacst.edu.sa/eDoc/2009/173799_1.pdf

Sloan, J., & Mackey, K. (2009). *Voise Academy: Pioneering a blended-learning model in a Chicago public high school.* San Mateo, CA: Innosight Institute. Retrieved from www.christenseninstitute.org/publications/voise-academy-pioneering-a-blended-learning-model-in-a-chicago-public-high-school/

Sparkes, R., & Williams, L. (2000). *Supporting learning: Ministerial panel on educational delivery in the classroom.* St. John's, NL: Queen's Printing for Newfoundland and Labrador.

Stevens, K. (1997). The place of telelearning in the development of rural schools in Newfoundland and Labrador. *Prospects, 4*(4). Retrieved from http://web.archive.org/web/20071017071819/http://www.cdli.ca/Community/Prospects/v4n4/telelearning.htm

Secretaría de Educación Básica. (2010). Enciclomedia Program. Iztacalco, MX: Author. Retrieved from www.sep.gob.mx/en/sep_en/Enciclomedia_program

Watson, J., Murin, A., Vashaw, L., Gemin, B., & Rapp, C. (2010). *Keeping pace with K–12 online learning: An annual review of policy and practice.* Durango, CO: Evergreen Education Group. Retrieved from www.kpk12.com/cms/wp-content/uploads/KeepingPaceK12_2010.pdf

Watson, J., Murin, A., Vashaw, L., Gemin, B., & Rapp, C. (2012). *Keeping pace with K–12 online & blended learning: An annual review of policy and practice.* Durango, CO: Evergreen Education Group. Retrieved from http://kpk12.com/cms/wp-content/uploads/KeepingPace2012.pdf

Watson, J., Murin, A., Vashaw, L., Gemin, B., & Rapp, C. (2013). *Keeping pace with K–12 online & blended learning: An annual review of policy and practice.* Durango, CO: Evergreen Education Group. Retrieved from http://kpk12.com/cms/wp-content/uploads/EEG_KP2013-lr.pdf

Watson, J. F., Winograd, K., & Kalmon, S. (2004). *Keeping pace with K–12 online learning: A snapshot of state-level policy and practice.* Naperville, IL: Learning Point Associates.

Wenmoth, D. (1996). Learning in the distributed classroom. *SET Research Information for Teachers, 2*(4), 1–4.

Winkelmans, T., Anderson, B., & Barbour, M. K. (2010). Distributed learning in British Columbia: A journey from correspondence to online delivery. *Journal of Open, Flexible and Distance Learning, 14*(1), 6–28. Retrieved from http://journals.akoaotearoa.ac.nz/index.php/JOFDL/article/viewFile/29/26

Wynne, S. D. (1997). *An overview of virtual schooling in North America and Europe.* Victoria, BC: Open Learning Age.

ISTE's National Educational Technology Standards

ISTE's NETS for Students (NETS·S)

All K–12 students should be prepared to meet the following standards and performance indicators.

1. **Creativity and Innovation**

   Students demonstrate creative thinking, construct knowledge, and develop innovative products and processes using technology. Students:

   a. apply existing knowledge to generate new ideas, products, or processes

   b. create original works as a means of personal or group expression

   c. use models and simulations to explore complex systems and issues

   d. identify trends and forecast possibilities

2. **Communication and Collaboration**

   Students use digital media and environments to communicate and work collaboratively, including at a distance, to support individual learning and contribute to the learning of others. Students:

   a. interact, collaborate, and publish with peers, experts, or others employing a variety of digital environments and media

   b. communicate information and ideas effectively to multiple audiences using a variety of media and formats

   c. develop cultural understanding and global awareness by engaging with learners of other cultures

   d. contribute to project teams to produce original works or solve problems

3. Research and Information Fluency

Students apply digital tools to gather, evaluate, and use information. Students:

a. plan strategies to guide inquiry

b. locate, organize, analyze, evaluate, synthesize, and ethically use information from a variety of sources and media

c. evaluate and select information sources and digital tools based on the appropriateness to specific tasks

d. process data and report results

4. Critical Thinking, Problem Solving, and Decision Making

Students use critical-thinking skills to plan and conduct research, manage projects, solve problems, and make informed decisions using appropriate digital tools and resources. Students:

a. identify and define authentic problems and significant questions for investigation

b. plan and manage activities to develop a solution or complete a project

c. collect and analyze data to identify solutions and make informed decisions

d. use multiple processes and diverse perspectives to explore alternative solutions

5. Digital Citizenship

Students understand human, cultural, and societal issues related to technology and practice legal and ethical behavior. Students:

a. advocate and practice the safe, legal, and responsible use of information and technology

b. exhibit a positive attitude toward using technology that supports collaboration, learning, and productivity

c. demonstrate personal responsibility for lifelong learning

d. exhibit leadership for digital citizenship

6. Technology Operations and Concepts

Students demonstrate a sound understanding of technology concepts, systems, and operations. Students:

a. understand and use technology systems

b. select and use applications effectively and productively

c. troubleshoot systems and applications

d. transfer current knowledge to the learning of new technologies

ISTE's NETS for Teachers (NETS·T)

All classroom teachers should be prepared to meet the following standards and performance indicators.

1. **Facilitate and Inspire Student Learning and Creativity**

   Teachers use their knowledge of subject matter, teaching and learning, and technology to facilitate experiences that advance student learning, creativity, and innovation in both face-to-face and virtual environments. Teachers:

   a. promote, support, and model creative and innovative thinking and inventiveness

   b. engage students in exploring real-world issues and solving authentic problems using digital tools and resources

   c. promote student reflection using collaborative tools to reveal and clarify students' conceptual understanding and thinking, planning, and creative processes

   d. model collaborative knowledge construction by engaging in learning with students, colleagues, and others in face-to-face and virtual environments

2. **Design and Develop Digital-Age Learning Experiences and Assessments**

   Teachers design, develop, and evaluate authentic learning experiences and assessments incorporating contemporary tools and resources to maximize content learning in context and to develop the knowledge, skills, and attitudes identified in the NETS·S. Teachers:

   a. design or adapt relevant learning experiences that incorporate digital tools and resources to promote student learning and creativity

   b. develop technology-enriched learning environments that enable all students to pursue their individual curiosities and become active participants in setting their own educational goals, managing their own learning, and assessing their own progress

   c. customize and personalize learning activities to address students' diverse learning styles, working strategies, and abilities using digital tools and resources

   d. provide students with multiple and varied formative and summative assessments aligned with content and technology standards and use resulting data to inform learning and teaching

3. **Model Digital-Age Work and Learning**

   Teachers exhibit knowledge, skills, and work processes representative of an innovative professional in a global and digital society. Teachers:

   a. demonstrate fluency in technology systems and the transfer of current knowledge to new technologies and situations

    b. collaborate with students, peers, parents, and community members using digital tools and resources to support student success and innovation

    c. communicate relevant information and ideas effectively to students, parents, and peers using a variety of digital-age media and formats

    d. model and facilitate effective use of current and emerging digital tools to locate, analyze, evaluate, and use information resources to support research and learning

4. Promote and Model Digital Citizenship and Responsibility

Teachers understand local and global societal issues and responsibilities in an evolving digital culture and exhibit legal and ethical behavior in their professional practices. Teachers:

    a. advocate, model, and teach safe, legal, and ethical use of digital information and technology, including respect for copyright, intellectual property, and the appropriate documentation of sources

    b. address the diverse needs of all learners by using learner-centered strategies and providing equitable access to appropriate digital tools and resources

    c. promote and model digital etiquette and responsible social interactions related to the use of technology and information

    d. develop and model cultural understanding and global awareness by engaging with colleagues and students of other cultures using digital-age communication and collaboration tools

5. Engage in Professional Growth and Leadership

Teachers continuously improve their professional practice, model lifelong learning, and exhibit leadership in their school and professional community by promoting and demonstrating the effective use of digital tools and resources. Teachers:

    a. participate in local and global learning communities to explore creative applications of technology to improve student learning

    b. exhibit leadership by demonstrating a vision of technology infusion, participating in shared decision making and community building, and developing the leadership and technology skills of others

    c. evaluate and reflect on current research and professional practice on a regular basis to make effective use of existing and emerging digital tools and resources in support of student learning

    d. contribute to the effectiveness, vitality, and self-renewal of the teaching profession and of their school and community

ISTE's NETS for Administrators (NETS·A)

All school administrators should be prepared to meet the following standards and performance indicators.

1. Visionary Leadership

Educational Administrators inspire and lead development and implementation of a shared vision for comprehensive integration of technology to promote excellence and support transformation throughout the organization. Educational Administrators:

   a. inspire and facilitate among all stakeholders a shared vision of purposeful change that maximizes use of digital-age resources to meet and exceed learning goals, support effective instructional practice, and maximize performance of district and school leaders

   b. engage in an ongoing process to develop, implement, and communicate technology-infused strategic plans aligned with a shared vision

   c. advocate on local, state, and national levels for policies, programs, and funding to support implementation of a technology-infused vision and strategic plan

2. Digital-Age Learning Culture

Educational Administrators create, promote, and sustain a dynamic, digital-age learning culture that provides a rigorous, relevant, and engaging education for all students. Educational Administrators:

   a. ensure instructional innovation focused on continuous improvement of digital-age learning

   b. model and promote the frequent and effective use of technology for learning

   c. provide learner-centered environments equipped with technology and learning resources to meet the individual, diverse needs of all learners

   d. ensure effective practice in the study of technology and its infusion across the curriculum

   e. promote and participate in local, national, and global learning communities that stimulate innovation, creativity, and digital-age collaboration

3. Excellence in Professional Practice

Educational Administrators promote an environment of professional learning and innovation that empowers educators to enhance student learning through the infusion of contemporary technologies and digital resources. Educational Administrators:

   a. allocate time, resources, and access to ensure ongoing professional growth in technology fluency and integration

    b. facilitate and participate in learning communities that stimulate, nurture, and support administrators, faculty, and staff in the study and use of technology

    c. promote and model effective communication and collaboration among stakeholders using digital-age tools

    d. stay abreast of educational research and emerging trends regarding effective use of technology and encourage evaluation of new technologies for their potential to improve student learning

4. Systemic Improvement

Educational Administrators provide digital-age leadership and management to continuously improve the organization through the effective use of information and technology resources. Educational Administrators:

    a. lead purposeful change to maximize the achievement of learning goals through the appropriate use of technology and media-rich resources

    b. collaborate to establish metrics, collect and analyze data, interpret results, and share findings to improve staff performance and student learning

    c. recruit and retain highly competent personnel who use technology creatively and proficiently to advance academic and operational goals

    d. establish and leverage strategic partnerships to support systemic improvement

    e. establish and maintain a robust infrastructure for technology including integrated, interoperable technology systems to support management, operations, teaching, and learning

5. Digital Citizenship

Educational Administrators model and facilitate understanding of social, ethical, and legal issues and responsibilities related to an evolving digital culture. Educational Administrators:

    a. ensure equitable access to appropriate digital tools and resources to meet the needs of all learners

    b. promote, model, and establish policies for safe, legal, and ethical use of digital information and technology

    c. promote and model responsible social interactions related to the use of technology and information

    d. model and facilitate the development of a shared cultural understanding and involvement in global issues through the use of contemporary communication and collaboration tools

Index

R

Radio WillowWeb, 33
role-playing, 45

S

SAM (successive approximation model), 4
SAM2 (extended successive approximation
     model), 4
schools
    brick-and-mortar, 55
    cyber, 55
    multi-district, 56
    single-district, 56
    virtual, 55
The Science Show for Kids, 33
Second Life
    about, 42, 43, 44
    challenges, 48
    educational potential, 44, 45, 46, 47
security, in virtual worlds, 48–49
self-assessments, 12–15
Sheehy, Peggy, 48
simulation, 46–47
Singapore, 54, 67–68, 70
single-district schools, 56
Skype, 27, 28
SlideShare, 24
South Korea, 68, 70
State of the Nation: K–12 Online Learning in
    Canada, 62
statewide supplemental programs, 56
Stone, David E., 46
storytelling, 45
successive approximation model (SAM), 4
Suffern Middle School, 45, 46
supplemental programs, statewide, 56
systematic design, 2–4
systemic thinking and action, 4–6

T

Tech Time with Mr. S, 33
technological applications. See also podcasting
    about, 19
    file storage/sharing, 26–27
    learning management systems, 20–22
    presentation sharing tools, 23–26
    voice-over-Internet protocol/web conferenc-
      ing tools, 27–28
    wikis, 22–23
text-based announcements, 16

thinking and action, systemic, 4–6
3DMee, 43
Turkey, 68–69, 70

U

United States K–12 online learning
    past, 57–58
    present, 54, 58–61, 69

V

variance, 2
video announcements, 16
videoconferences, 18
Virtual High School (VHS) Global Consortium,
    58
Virtual Learning Network, 66–67
virtual schools, 55
virtual worlds
    about, 42–44
    avatars, 43
    challenges, 48–49
    educational potential, 44–47
    learning curve, 48
    pornography/inappropriate content, 48
    security, 48–49
    statistics, 42
    tools, 43
    visually impaired, access for, 48
visually impaired, access to virtual worlds, 48
voice-over-Internet protocol, 27–28
Voise Academy, 55

W

web conferencing tools, 27–28
wikis, 22–23